A Journal of the American Civil War

Editor:

Theodore P. Savas

VOLUME FIVE

NUMBER TWO

Published quarterly by Regimental Studies, Inc., a nonprofit charitable corporation

Subscription and General Information

Civil War Regiments is published quarterly by Regimental Studies, Inc., a nonprofit charitable corporation located at 1475 South Bascom Avenue, Suite 204, Campbell, CA 95008. Editor: Theodore P. Savas. Voice: (408) 879-9073; Facsimile: 408-879-9327; E-Mail: MHBooks@aol.com

Trade and newsstand distribution is handled by Peter Rossi at Stackpole Books, 5067 Ritter Road, Mechanicsburg, PA 17055-6921. Voice: 1-800-732-3669; Fax: 1-717-976-0412. Dealer inquires welcome.

SUBSCRIPTIONS: $29.95/year, ppd (four books), individual and institutional. Back issues may be ordered from the publisher. Write to: Back Issues, CWR, 1475 South Bascom, Suite 204, Campbell, CA 95008, or call 1-800-848-6585, for pricing information, contents and availability. Please specify the volume and issue number when placing your order. Prepayment with check, money order, or MC/V is required. Two hundred and fifty signed and numbered four-issue Collector's Sets for the premier volume were printed. Cost is $40.00 ppd. Inquire as to availability. FOREIGN ORDERS: Subscriptions: $35.95/year, including surface delivery. Payment in United States currency only or MC/V. Allow eight to twelve weeks for delivery.

MANUSCRIPTS AND CORRESPONDENCE: We welcome manuscript inquiries. For author's guidelines, send a self-addressed, double-stamped business envelope to: CWR-Editor, 1475 South Bascom, Suite 204, Campbell, CA 95008. Include a brief description of your proposed topic and the sources to be utilized. No unsolicited submissions will be returned without proper postage. Book review inquiries or submissions should be directed to Dr. Archie McDonald, Book Review Editor, Stephen F. Austin University, Department of History, P.O. Box 6223, SFA Station, Nacogdoches, Texas 75962-6223. (409) 568-2407. Enclose a self-addressed-stamped-envelope if requesting a reply.

This journal is printed on 50-lb. J.B. Offset recycled, acid-free paper

Thanks to your support, *Civil War Regiments* has been able to make a number of donations to Civil War-related preservation organizations. Some of the recipients of these donations are listed below:

(LIFE MEMBER) ASSOCIATION FOR THE PRESERVATION OF CIVIL WAR SITES

RICHARD B. GARNETT MEMORIAL , HOLLYWOOD CEMETERY

HERITAGEPAC / CIVIL WAR ROUND TABLE ASSOCIATES

SAVE HISTORIC ANTIETAM FOUNDATION / TURNER ASHBY HOUSE, PORT REPUBLIC, VA

THE COKER HOUSE RESTORATION PROJECT, JACKSON, MS CWRT

AMERICAN BLUE & GRAY ASSOCIATION

APCWS 1993 MALVERN HILL/GLENDALE CAMPAIGN

Civil War Regiments, Vol. 5, No. 2, Copyright 1996

by Regimental Studies, Inc.

ISBN 1-882810-52-X

STATEMENT OF PURPOSE: Regimental Studies, Inc., is a non-partisan, non-profit charitable corporation founded to further two specific goals. First, it is hoped that Civil War Regiments will encourage further research into the often neglected area of unit history studies by providing a serial outlet for that research. It is also our intent to raise funds for the preservation and protection of endangered Civil War sites by donating proceeds to various preservation organizations, when it is possible for us to do so. To this end, your active support in the form of donations, advertisements, articles and subscriptions, is both encouraged and welcomed. Thank you.

Contributors:

Stephen E. Wise, a historian living in Beaufort, South Carolina, is the director of the Parris Island Marine Corps Museum and author of *Lifeline of the Confederacy: Block-ade Running During the Civil War* (Columbia, 1989). He received his Ph.D. from the University of South Carolina, and teaches history as an adjunct professor at his alma mater.

Steven D. Smith is a Consulting Archaeologist with the South Carolina Institute of Archaeology and Anthropology. He holds a B.A. in history from the Virginia Military Institute and a Master's from the University of Kentucky. The South Carolina Department of Archives and History is gratefully thanked for permission to use portions of *Whom We Would Never More See* (Topics in African American History 3, South Carolina Department of Archives and History, Columbia, SC, 1993) in this article. For further information on the archaeological excavations described herein, see James B. Legg and Steven D. Smith, *"The Best Ever Occupied. . . ." Archaeological Excavations of a Civil War Encampment on Folly Island* (South Carolina Institute of Archaeology and Anthropology, Research Manuscript Series 209, Columbia, SC, 1989).

Patrick Brennan, a graduate of Loyola University, is a nationally known music pro-ducer and composer. Active in the advertising industry, he is the owner of two Chicago-based businesses, Hubbard Street Productions and Hubbard Street Studios. Brennan, a life-long student of the Civil War, recently released his first book, *Secessionville: Assault on Charleston* (Savas Publishing Co., 1996).

Jeffrey T. Ryan holds a Master's Degree in history from Temple University in Phila-delphia, where he is completing work on a Ph.D. Ryan is the 1992 Dissertation Fellow of the Marine Corps Historical Foundation, and is currently conducting research for a history of the Civil War-era Marine Corps.

Theodore P. Savas is an attorney in Campbell, California, and founder of *Civil War Regiments*. He is an avid student of the American Civil War and military history. His new book on a more recent conflict, *Silent Hunters: German U-Boat Commanders of World War II*, will be released in the spring of 1997.

 A Journal of the American Civil War

Table of Contents

Introduction

Theodore P. Savas

S outh Carolina's importance to the Confederacy and her significant role in the origins of secession and civil war were manifest. Federal combined military operations along her numerous inlets and semi-tropical shorelines were as interesting as they were complex. Charleston—the appropriately-titled "Cradle of the Confederacy,"—was for years the objective of a determined and well-equipped enemy. Indeed, the critical seaport would stand defiant against all comers until flanked by William T. Sherman's army in February 1865, just two months before Appomattox.

The personalities that labored within her borders were as fascinating and multi-faceted as the military events they had a hand in crafting. Confederate defenders included men of wildly divergent abilities, including Robert E. "Granny" Lee, who used his brilliant engineering talents to bolster the region's defenses before being recalled to Richmond—and immortality; John Pemberton, the enigmatic Pennsylvanian, who managed to ward off the first Federal attempt to capture Charleston before traveling west to lose Vicksburg to U. S. Grant; the mercurial and vain P. G. T. Beauregard, who loathed only the Confederate president more than his assignment to what he believed was a inferior post of command; and the piercing eyed rapscallion Nathan "Shanks" Evans, whose personal staff included his own "barellita," a bottomless keg of hard liquor.

The Federals who traveled south with conquest in their hearts also boasted a wide assortment of characters, including the redoubtable Admiral Samuel Francis Du Pont, who realized far earlier than his superiors the vulnerabilities of ironclad monitors against stationary forts; Isaac Stevens, the stubbornly-competent general whose men were slaughtered before an earthen fort on the orders of a bumbling politico; the calculating engineer Quincy Gillmore, who failed to match his success at Fort Pulaski in Georgia; and the thoroughly detestable David Hunter, a conniving and devious individual even Robert E. Lee found distasteful.

And yet, despite having hosted a plethora of incredible events dictated by the likes of these men—events that even fiction writers would be hard-pressed to spawn—little scholarly attention has been devoted to the study of military operations in South Carolina. Thankfully, there are several talented and enthusiastic historians and writers that have taken a collective hand in beginning to unlock the tales that remain to be told about the war along the southeastern Atlantic seaboard. Some of them grace the pages of this unique compendium of essays.

Historian Stephen R. Wise opens this issue of *Civil War Regiments* with "To Capture an Island: Amphibious Operations in the Department of the South, 1861-1865," an insightful examination into combined operations in the theater. Dr. Wise, the Marine Corps historian at Parris Island, is no stranger to Civil War South Carolina. His two previous books relating to this theater, *Lifeline of the Confederacy* (Columbia, 1988) and *Gate of Hell: Campaign for Charleston Harbor, 1863* (Columbia, 1994), are recognized as outstanding original contributions to the literature. Indeed few historians know more about the war along the Palmetto state's coast than Wise.

While even those with a passing interest in the Civil War have heard of the 54th Massachusetts Infantry or seen the movie *Glory* (which depicts the black regiment's forlorn assault against Battery Wagner), almost no one is familiar with its sister regiment, the all-black 55th Massachusetts Infantry. When human remains were accidentally uncovered on Folly Island several years ago, Steven D. Smith, an archaeologist with the South Carolina Institute of Archaeology and Anthropology, was one of a handful of scientists brought in to investigate. The result of his in-depth field and archival research is "History and Archaeology: Edward Wild's African Brigade in the Siege of Charleston." The monograph sheds considerable light on the fascinating—and tragic—story of how these soldiers lived and died on Folly Island during the siege of Charleston. "History and Archaeology" deals with a variety of political, military and social issues—and one riveting mystery: why were so many of the skeletal remains missing skulls?

The first serious attempt to capture Charleston ended on James Island with a stinging defeat for the Federals on June 16, 1862 at Secessionville. Events leading up to that engagement included a little-known reconnaissance and battle thirteen days earlier, the subject of Patrick Brennan's essay "Prelude to Secessionville: First Blood on Sol Legare Island." This brisk affair, typical of many of the engagements fought on the barrier islands, was hard-fought, poorly-managed and ultimately, inconclusive. Brennan, a nationally-known Chicago-based composer and musician, is the author of the recent *Secessionville: Assault on Charleston* (Campbell, CA, 1996), the first full-length treatment of this important early war battle that helped shape the three-year Federal siege of Charleston. "First Blood" is adapted from that work.

Closing out this assemblage of articles is "To the Shores of Carolina: Admiral Dahlgren's Marine Battalions," by Jeffrey Ryan. A 1992 Dissertation Fellow of the Marine Corps Historical Foundation, Ryan explains the difficulties commanders encountered in properly utilizing this special service branch while recounting the marine battalions' outstanding—and often overlooked—service. Dr. Ryan is currently researching a complete history of the role of Civil War-era marines.

It is hoped that the work presented by these authors will foster additional interest and support for further study of the war along the southeastern Atlantic seaboard, for much yet remains to be explored.

To CAPTURE AN ISLAND:
Amphibious Operations in the Department of the South, 1861-1863

Stephen R. Wise

A mphibious operations have always been an important part of military strategy. Throughout the ages the transportation and landing of military forces by maritime vessels has been essential to achieving victory. Drawing on the experience of others, Americans carried out amphibious operations during the Colonial Wars, the Revolution and the War of 1812. During the Mexican War, future Civil War leaders saw first hand at Vera Cruz and Tampico the advantage gained by a successful combination of naval and land forces.

During the Civil War, Northern forces carried out a number of campaigns that could be termed "amphibious operations." One area where such coordinated missions occurred was the South Carolina coast, where attacks involving land and naval forces were used against Confederate positions. Three important amphibious operations occurred between November 1861 and September 1863: the November 7, 1861, attack and occupation of Hilton Head Island; the July 10, 1863, attack on Morris Island; and the September 8, 1863, assault on Fort Sumter. Each campaign produced insights as to how amphibious assaults should be carried out. To examine these battles and explain why they succeeded or failed, one can apply the formula set forth by the Civil War commander Brig. Gen. Egbert Viele, USA, who stated that "the three principles that govern a true plan of military operations are secrecy, celerity and audacity." Since all three of the

Adm. Francis Du Pont
North Atlantic Blockading Squadron

Marine Corps Recruit Depot, Parris Island, SC

assaults mentioned above were combined operations between the navy and the army, a fourth factor, joint service cooperation, should likewise be examined.[1]

At the beginning of the Civil War Northern leaders agreed in principle to a strategy that was formulated to reduce and eventually break the South's ability to wage war. Along the coast this translated into a blockade that was designed to stop overseas supplies from reaching the Confederacy. To effectively blockade the coast, the Federals needed secure coaling stations along the Southern coastline. To seize and establish such bases required joint expeditions, and one of the first operations was directed against the South Carolina coast. On October 12, 1861, confidential orders were sent to Capt. Samuel Francis Du Pont directing him to make a lodgment along the Southern coast and establish a base for the South Atlantic Blockading Squadron. By the end of the month, Du Pont had decided to seize Port Royal Sound, South Carolina. As he wrote: "Port Royal alone admits the large ships—and gives us such a naval position on the seacoast of the enemy as our Army is holding across the Potomac."[2]

To capture Port Royal, Du Pont was given command of a joint army-navy expedition charged with defeating an unknown enemy force and ordered to occupy a large area in the midst of hostile territory. This was not an easy task, but Du Pont worked hard to meet the needed elements of a successful amphibious operation. With assistance from his superiors, Du Pont brought together the largest naval force ever assembled by the United States up to this time. It consisted of 17 warships, 25 coaling vessels and 33 transports. On board the transports were 13,000 soldiers under the command of Brig. Gen. Thomas W. Sherman, and a battalion of Marines.[3]

Though he regularly conferred with General Sherman, Du Pont was the overall commander and was responsible for the expedition's success or failure. Du Pont also carefully evaluated his resources. He had the potential to launch a huge amphibious operation, but the naval commander looked warily upon the expedition's ability to carry out a successful landing. Though he had confidence in his sailors, naval officers and warships, he doubted the ability of the soldiers and marines. As he candidly wrote: ". . .soldiers and marines are the most helpless people I ever saw."[4]

From the outset Du Pont did not want to carry out a landing. Instead, he planned to defeat the Confederates by employing only his warships. Du Pont's instructions from Secretary of the Navy Gideon Welles gave him the authority needed to keep the army from taking part. Welles acknowledged to Du Pont that, even though the flag officer and General Sherman were supposed to cooperate, as long as the soldiers were onboard ships they were to be considered as Marines.

As such, Du Pont's authority over them took precedence over Sherman's. Still, being a diplomatic gentleman, Du Pont kept his intentions from his joint commander and even allowed the army to practice their landing techniques—even though he planned never to use them. As Du Pont confided to his wife:

> At Port Royal the soldiers will have nothing to do—they are obliterated—though we did work out a distant landing for them when we investigated the subject; whether Sherman will agree to be a looker-on is another element. I am supreme in the decision, it is true, but it may be very unwise to act. If we can take, we hold. With soldiers it would be very doubtful, for great forces could be brought to bear upon them—upon us only forts, which we would not allow them to put up.[5]

The expedition sailed from Hampton Roads on October 29, 1861, and only Du Pont and certain key officials in the Navy Department knew of its ultimate destination. Secrecy, one of the elements needed for a successful attack, was vital, and it was not until the force was at sea did Du Pont reveal the destination to his commanders and the army officers. By keeping the objective secret, the Federals kept their enemy off balance. The Confederates were well aware of the fleet's departure but they were unaware of its exact target, so while garrisons throughout South Carolina, Georgia and Florida were placed on alert, the Southerners were unable to concentrate their forces at any one point.

The expedition almost ended before it began when the fleet encountered a tremendous gale off Cape Hatteras, North Carolina. Four ships were sunk and the squadron scattered, but individually they began to re-assemble off Port Royal Sound and by November 3, the majority of the squadron had arrived. Du Pont began making his final plans for capturing Port Royal. Opposing the Union force at the mouth of Port Royal Sound were two well-built but widely separated earthen forts. The largest of the pair was Fort Walker, located on Hilton Head Island, while across the sound on Bay Point was the smaller Fort Beauregard. The well-armed forts mounted nearly 50 guns, but because of the large size of the sound, neither bastion could support the other. As a result, the Federals could close on and attack one bastion and be out of range of the other.[6]

Du Pont realized this flaw in the Confederate defense and made preparations to attack Fort Walker. The flag officer still intended to keep it a naval affair. General Sherman, however, proposed a landing on Hilton Head while the navy kept the forts under a hot fire. Although Du Pont believed the maneuver fraught with danger, he luckily avoided any confrontation over the issue because certain key vessels needed to land the soldiers were still unaccounted for. Among the absent vessels were the ferryboats, all but one tug and the sailing ship *Ocean Express*, which contained the army's small arms ammunition and artillery. Without these essentials, a landing was out of the question. Also absent was the battalion of marines, whose transport sank during the storm. Although the marines were rescued, the ship that had picked them up, the sailing frigate *Sabine*, had not yet reached Port Royal. At the same time Du Pont realized that the longer he waited, the stronger his enemy would become. Because of these factors, it was decided to go in with the warships.[7]

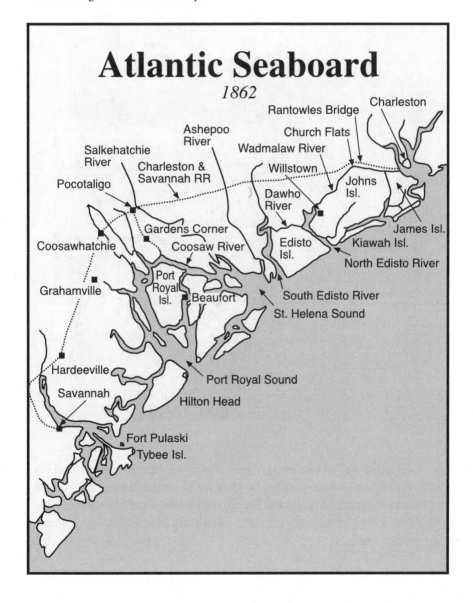

Union Troops Land After the Battle of Port Royal.

Harper's Weekly

On November 7, 1861, in one of the first battles fought between fortifications and steam-powered warships, Du Pont, on board his flagship *Wabash*, led his vessels into the sound and silenced Fort Walker. The smothering fire from the ships forced the Confederate garrison to flee Hilton Head Island. To guarantee that the navy received full credit for the victory, Du Pont made sure that the first people ashore were sailors. Commander John Rodgers of Du Pont's staff raised the United States flag over Fort Walker, and Capt. Christopher R. P. Rodgers, together with the marines from the *Wabash*, occupied the fort. Only then did the navy allow the army to land, and at sunset Fort Walker was turned over to General Sherman and his men.[8]

Even though there was no landing of ground forces, the attack on Port Royal Sound met the elements of a successful amphibious operation. First, the expedition retained its secrecy and kept the enemy from reinforcing the point of attack. Second, the expedition developed quickly: only ten days passed from the time the squadron sailed from Hampton Roads to the capitulation of Fort Walker. Lastly, Du Pont's movement was especially audacious since the assault was launched deep in enemy territory against a force of unknown size. While the officers who sailed together on the *Wabash* enjoyed each others' company, communications between the joint commands was a problem. If General Sherman had pressed Du Pont to land his men, the flag officer would probably have denied his request and evoked his instructions from Welles to treat the soldiers as marines as long as they were onboard the ships. Certainly strained relations between the two leaders might have occurred, but circumstances kept any confrontation from happening. Thus, no precedent for joint command was set at Port Royal and, since the attack was a complete victory, the issue was never addressed in after-action reports.

For the next year and a half, Federal operations along the southeastern coast followed the same pattern set at Port Royal: there were no amphibious landings. Instead the navy, under now Rear Adm. Du Pont, would clear the way and the army would come ashore. This style of operation continued until July 1863, when new commanders, tasked with capturing Charleston, South Carolina, arrived in the Department of the South. The new officers were Rear Adm. John A. Dahlgren and Maj. Gen. Quincy A. Gillmore. The details for the Charleston campaign had been worked out in Washington before the two officers traveled south. Both Dahlgren and Gillmore realized that in order to capture Charleston, the city's main bastion of Fort Sumter had to be neutralized. The fort, a large masonry work built on a shoal at the mouth of the harbor, controlled the main ship channel. Northern warships could not enter the harbor until Fort Sumter was rendered ineffective. To do this, Dahlgren and Gillmore agreed that an attack against Morris Island, a low-lying barrier island located just south of Fort Sumter, was necessary. After Morris Island was taken, the army could construct breaching batteries on Cummings Point, the northern tip of the island, and thereby destroy or neutralize Fort Sumter. Once the fort was no longer a threat to Federal ships, the navy could enter the harbor.[9] For the attack on Morris Island, the Federals

Maj. Gen. Quincy Gillmore

Generals in Blue

improved their base on Folly Island, a barrier island located southeast of Morris Island.

The two islands were separated by a small body of water known locally as Lighthouse Inlet. Before Gillmore's appearance on Folly Island, the rival pickets freely communicated and traded goods across the inlet; once the new commander arrived, all fraternization was prohibited. On the Confederate side of the inlet, Oyster Point, Southerners had built a strong set of detached batteries mounting eleven guns and mortars, all supported by a line of rifle pits. Stationed in these works were approximately 175 artillerymen and 450 infantrymen.[10]

Unlike the attack on Port Royal, army commander Gillmore had no intention of taking a secondary role in the move against Morris Island. Gillmore, a veteran of Atlantic coastal operations, took the lead in planning the assault, leaving the navy to assume a supporting role. His attack plan was a bold one. It called for a two-pronged amphibious night assault on Morris Island under the cover of a naval and land bombardment. His assault force, stationed aboard navy launches, was to proceed through Light-house Creek, a tidal waterway that ran along the landside of Folly Island, to Lighthouse In-

Rear Adm. John A. Dahlgren
North Atlantic Blockading
Squadron

National Archives

let. There, the flotilla was to split in half, with one section moving directly against the Confederate lines at Oyster Point, and the other continuing through inland creeks to a landing point in the middle of Morris Island. To cover the landing against Oyster Point, Gillmore's men secretly constructed a line of masked batteries on the northern tip of Folly Island directly across from the Confederate works. Gillmore also coordinated with Admiral Dahlgren for the use of the navy's ironclads in a joint bombardment of Morris Island. At the same time, Gillmore requested that Dahlgren furnish the landing force, a 2,000-man brigade under the command of Brig. Gen. George C. Strong, with small boats.[11]

Dahlgren readily agreed to Gillmore's plan and on July 7 ordered the tug *Dandelion* to debark from Port Royal with the necessary small boats and proceed with "great secrecy" to Folly Island. The *Dandelion* and the tug *0. M. Petit* took on the role of mother ships to a flock of naval launches. The launches were armed with the Dahlgren boat howitzer, a bronze weapon designed by Dahlgren to provide cover fire for coastal landings. The entire force was commanded by Lt. Cmdr. Francis M. Bunce.

The operation was not without some risk, for neither Gillmore nor Dahlgren knew with any degree of certainty the strength of the Confederate forces defending Charleston. Although he had no exact figures, Gillmore was convinced that he was outnumbered. In order to mask his attack on Morris island and stop enemy reinforcements from reaching Charleston, Gillmore planned two simultaneous diversions in conjunction with the landing on Morris Island. While these maneuvers weakened his primary attacking force, Gillmore felt confident that he would be able to quickly seize Morris Island. In reality, however, with fifty percent of his force committed to the diversions, Gillmore was greatly reducing the manpower he needed to take Morris Island.[12]

The twin-prong night attack was initially scheduled for July 9, but preparations were not completed in time. As a result, Gillmore modified both his plan and the time of the assault to July 10.[13] Gillmore's revised scheme was less complicated and therefore less dangerous. Justifiably concerned that the Confederates may have been forewarned, he called off the two-pronged night assault and cancelled the landing in the middle of Morris Island. Instead, the Union commander decided to strike a concentrated blow on the Southern end of the island. By employing superior firepower from both his batteries and Dahlgren's ships, Gillmore was certain that he could silence the Confederate works and land Strong's Brigade at daylight, directly under the Confederate guns. Once ashore, Gillmore believed that Strong's Federals would quickly overrun the Southern batteries and take the entire island in one day. In this new scenario, the battle would depend largely on the power and the ability of the opposing artillery and gunners. In this realm Gillmore and Dahlgren had complete confidence in their superiority.[14]

This time the Union movement proceeded according to plan. At 9:00 p.m. on July 9, Strong's brigade marched to the west side of Folly Island, where the launches were waiting to take them to Morris Island. With the 7th Connecticut Infantry in the lead boats, Strong's brigade proceeded up the river. Unskilled at handling cutters the men did not row in unison, causing one soldier to remark later that it was as if there were "forty different tides running in as many directions." The small flotilla of boats proceeded according to plan enveloped in silence, the only noises being a hushed officer's voice, muffled oars and alligators occasionally plunging into the water. By early morning on July 10, the flotilla reached Lighthouse Inlet and positioned itself in the tall grass lining the waterway. Lieutenant Commander Bunce stationed his armed launches across the inlet, waiting for daylight when the attack was scheduled to begin. Unfortunately for the soldiers, a slight breeze and the currents in the river required that they row continuously to maintain their vessels' positions. While doing this, many of them pondered the task ahead, disliking the prospect of facing Confederate batteries in open boats.[15]

As morning neared General Truman Seymour, the overall commander of the attack, impatiently walked among the Union batteries. To gain tactical surprise, it was crucial that the Union guns open first. Seymour ordered his guns unmasked. It was still too dark for the Union gunners to make out their targets, but Seymour hoped by the time the obstructions were cleared from the gun ports, sufficient light would be available. In less than an hour the batteries were unmasked. The Confederate works were visible and at 5:08 a.m., Seymour ordered the batteries to commence firing.[16]

The morning of July 10 dawned fair. There was little or no breeze and the air hung hot and heavy. Though they were aware of the increased enemy activity, the Confederates had not broken their routine. No extra men had been posted and the soldiers at the batteries were just beginning to eat breakfast when Seymour's 32 rifled guns and 15 mortars interrupted their solitude. As the first shells fell on their positions, the Confederate drummers sounded the long roll and artillerymen rushed to their guns while the supporting infantry of the 21st and 1st South Carolina hurried to rifle pits in front and to the right of the batteries. Even though it was early morning, the extreme heat forced most of the Confederates to go to battle stripped to the waist.

The duel between the batteries continued for over an hour, with neither side gaining an advantage. The Union soldiers watched from their boats while they waited for Strong's signal to move forward. As they observed the contest, the men saw something that caused them to disregard their orders to maintain silence—the appearance of the Northern monitors on the Confederate flank. Cheers erupted from the launches as the naval warships added their heavy guns to the weight of the bombardment.[17]

On board the monitor *Catskill*, Dahlgren was bringing his flagship and her sister ships, the monitors *Nahant*, *Montauk* and *Weehawken* into action. As previously arranged with Gillmore, the admiral was moving in to flank the Confederate batteries. Using primarily shrapnel and grape from their 11-inch and 15-inch guns, the monitors fired their loads at a high elevation so the projectiles scattered over hundreds of yards, ripping through the Southern batteries.[18]

The effect of the monitors' guns on the battle was seen plainly by the men of Strong's brigade. The fire from the Confederate batteries, enfiladed by the ironclads, tapered off and became erratic. The lessening of enemy fire caused the Union soldiers to cheer even more loudly, which drew the attention of the Confederate gunners. Their position revealed, Lieutenant Commander Bunce returned fire using the boat guns in his cutters as he began to maneuver his men toward Morris Island. By now all available artillery pieces had entered into the fight.[19]

Despite being flanked by heavy fire from the monitors and smothered by incoming rounds from the boat howitzers, the Confederate artillerymen managed to lob a few shells toward the approaching launches. One of these vessels was sunk and General Strong's lead boat came dangerously close to being destroyed. As their exposed position became readily apparent, anxiety mounted in the barges, the men unable to answer the Confederate shells. One soldier remarked that he did not mind being killed or drowned; it was the possibility of both that bothered him, as he was wedged in so tight that he could "neither pray, fight nor swear."

The Union soldiers, through a hail of bursting shells, slowly worked their launches closer to Morris Island. Leading the way was the 7th Connecticut, followed by the 6th Connecticut, 3rd New Hampshire, 76th Pennsylvania, 9th Maine and 48th New York. As the distance to Morris Island shortened, the Federals found that the Southerners could not depress their guns enough to strike the launches, their shells whistling harmlessly overhead. It was but a temporary reprieve, however, for the Confederates manning the rifle pits began peppering the on-coming boats with concentrated musketry fire.[20]

When the water was shallow enough to support his men, Strong ordered the troops ashore against the rifle pits. Five of the six regiments obeyed the command and, with bayonets fixed, clamored out of their boats into the muddy water. Colonel Chatfield's 6th Connecticut, however, did not follow suit. Instead, Chatfield altered the course of his regiments' boats into Lighthouse Inlet where, taking advantage of the Confederates' inability to depress their cannon, he led his regiment toward the ocean.

While Chatfield's men were pulling away, regiment after regiment formed in knee deep mud and began wading inland. Strong, anxious to join his men, leaped from his boat before it landed and promptly disappeared under the water. The drenched colonel managed to surface and reach shore soon thereafter, where he took control of the ensuing assault. The Northerners advanced and soon the lead regiment, the 7th Connecticut, gained the rifle pits, where heavy hand-to-hand fighting took place. Without warning the Confederate defense suddenly collapsed and the Southerners began a hurried retreat.

The quick departure of the Confederate infantry was caused by the appearance of Chatfield's 6th Connecticut in the batteries above them. Having slipped under the enemy's guns, Chatfield landed his men above the batteries on the ocean side of Morris Island and led them in a charge against the rear and flanks of the Confederate works. For a short time the artillerymen resisted, but muskets and bayonets soon overwhelmed ramrods and spikes. The batteries were taken and the Union soldiers pushed on to surround the rifle pits. Sensing disaster and probable surrender, the Confederate commanders ordered a retreat that quickly degenerated into a rout. Chatfield and Strong united their forces, capturing a number of Confederates in the process. Those who managed to escape the envelopment streamed down Morris Island toward Battery Wagner, a Confederate fortification three miles distant. Using Wagner as a rallying point, the Southern commanders held their ground and brought up reinforcements.[21]

While the morning's events demoralized the Confederates, the Northerners were elated. The Union commanders, Strong mounted on a mule and Chatfield waving a captured Confederate flag, directed their men to follow the retreating enemy. The Northern soldiers were inspired by the discovery of newspapers in the captured works telling of Union victories at Gettysburg and Vicksburg. Lieutenant Colonel John Bedel of the 3rd New Hampshire ran among the advancing soldiers with a newspaper in one hand and his hat in another, crying "Vicksburg captured; Great victory at Gettysburg!" The men responded by cheering and charging towards Wagner.

But even this news could not push the exhausted men further. The heat was becoming unbearable and the Union soldiers found themselves dodging solid shot from rifled cannon mounted on Fort Sumter's gorge wall. The shots killed a few Union soldiers and a near miss buried some officers of the 3rd New Hampshire in the sand, wounding Lieutenant Colonel Bedel. As the column approached Battery Wagner the fortification's guns opened upon them, scattering the leading Federals with a terrible storm of grape and canister. The attacking force could do no more, its momentum bloodily blunted. The exhausted men halted the assault, with many of them falling in the sand to rest. Commanders quickly organized a picket line across the island and awaited orders.[22]

The Federal attack on Morris Island was an unqualified tactical success. Though some may argue that the landing resembled a river crossing more than a traditional amphibious expedition, Gillmore and Dahlgren had carried out the war's first successful operation where troops had gone ashore directly under enemy fire. By employing superior mass, firepower and surprise, the Federals were able to meet the requirements of a successful amphibious assault. Even though the Confederates realized that their Federals were planning an attack, they did not know the exact date and were caught off guard by not only the timing of the attack but also by its force. The placing of an entire infantry brigade in lightly armed boats directly under the guns of enemy batteries was an audacious move on Gillmore's part. If it had not worked, it would have been termed foolhardy; but Gillmore's boldness helped ensure the attack's success. In addition, cooperation between the two services was excellent. The long hours of planning had provided for a smooth operation that followed Gillmore's precise plans.

The only legitimate criticism is that the attack failed to capture the entire island. The Federals had no reserves, so even though they were able to overrun the Confederate batteries and take two-thirds of the island, the men were too exhausted to press on and capture Battery Wagner and the rest of Morris Island. If an additional force had been available, Gillmore could have used them on July 10 to overwhelm Wagner but, with half his command committed to diversions, there was no reserve on hand to press home the advantage. Instead, the attack stalled and the Confederates were able to regroup and bring in reinforcements. The next morning, when Gillmore sent Strong's brigade against the stronghold, the Northerners were easily repulsed.[23]

A week later Gillmore and Dahlgren used a rush of troops in a second attempt to capture Wagner on the evening of July 18. Unfortunately for the Federals, this attack also failed and the campaign on Morris Island settled into siege warfare. During the siege some amphibious assaults were contemplated against the remaining Confederate works on Morris Island, but neither Dahlgren or Gillmore were confident enough to undertake one. During the siege, Gillmore constructed breaching batteries in the center of Morris Island that destroyed Fort Sumter as an artillery position. The Confederates countered this achievement by using Sumter as an anchor for lines of obstructions and torpedoes (mines) that were placed in the channel. Eventually the Northern siege lines inched their way forward and on September 7, 1863, reached Battery Wagner's moat, forcing the Confederates to evacuate Morris Island.[24]

The capture of Morris Island encouraged the Northern commanders to carry out one final amphibious operation against Fort Sumter. Both Gillmore and Dahlgren realized that the Confederate fortification had to be taken in order to clear the main channel of obstructions. Unlike their joint operation against Morris Island however, this time there was very little cooperation between the two services. The long campaign on Morris Island had strained the working relationship between Dahlgren and Gillmore, and the stress between the two men affected the chances of success for an amphibious assault against Fort Sumter.

At first the Federals hoped to avoid a direct attack. On September 7, 1863, Dahlgren sent a note to the Confederate high command in Charleston demanding Sumter's surrender. The Southerners responded by inviting the admiral to come and take it. Spurred on by Confederate boastfulness, Dahlgren immediately initiated his movement by sending the monitor *Weehawken* into the shallow channel that ran between Fort Sumter and Cummings Point. In its effort to sever the fort's communications however, the *Weehawken* found itself unable to negotiate the channel and ran aground. She managed to float free at the next high tide and was promptly recalled from her exposed position. Despite the *Weehawken's* failure, Dahlgren decided to push his luck and ordered a small boat attack for the night of September 8.[25]

Unknown to Dahlgren, General Gillmore was also readying his boat infantry for an attack on Fort Sumter. The two commanders learned of each others' plans when they requested support from one another. Dahlgren asked for the return of four naval launches that had been serving with the army's amphibious unit, while Gillmore called upon Dahlgren to place his force under army command. Throughout the day messages were sent between Morris Island and Dahlgren's flagship in an effort to smooth out the obvious command wrinkles, but in the end the two officers refused to cooperate with each other. An exasperated Gillmore finally signalled Dahlgren:

> You decline to act in concert with me or allow the senior officer to command the assault on Sumter, but insist that a naval officer must command the party. Why this should be so in assaulting a fortification, I can not see. I am so fearful that some accident will take place between our parties that I would recall my own if it were not too late.
>
> I sent you the watchword by special messenger, who has returned. We must trust to chance and hope for the best. No matter who gets the fort if we place our flag over it.[26]

The two services went on with their preparations. Gillmore organized an assault force of about 500 men from the 10th Connecticut and the 24th Massachusetts under the latter regiment's Col. Francis A. Osborn. The regiments were to be transported on barges manned by the army's boat infantry—100 oarsmen from the 7th Connecticut under Maj. Oliver S. Sanford. The army's plan called for the vessels to come out of the tidal creeks near Cummings Point and land on Sumter's gorge and left flank.

The navy's plan was a bit more elaborate. Dahlgren ordered an assault force of 500 marines and sailors assembled on launches which were to be towed toward Fort Sumter by the tug *Dandelion*. Once abreast the fort the launches were to be cast loose, a portion carrying out a diversion against Sumter's right face while the others landed on the fort's right flank.

Though planned for the same night and the same time, there was no coordination between the two forces, though the two commanders agreed to use the password "Detroit" should the two expeditions become entangled. Gillmore, fearful of complications, ordered Colonel Osborn to turn back if the navy landed first.[27]

The operation was a disaster. The navy attacked first and even though they were within striking distance, Colonel Osborn reluctantly obeyed his orders and commanded his boats to turn back. In the darkness the naval officers in charge of the launches became disoriented and confused. Only one quarter of the landing force ever reached Sumter's brick-encrusted shoreline. The Confederates, who had broken the Federal code and had read Dahlgren's messages to Gillmore, were well prepared for the attack. The fort's commander, Maj. Stephen Elliott, had his 300-man garrison positioned around Sumter's walls outfitted as "sentries, grenadiers, turpentine-ballers and keg-flingers."

The best summation of the attack comes from a letter written by Major Elliott to his sister:

I kept the men quiet until two boats had nearly touched the landing place. Our fire then opened pretty sharply the enemy returning it from his outer boats in a very musical manner which made some of the boys keep time with their heads with more appreciation than pluck. Other detachments now came up and poured in a rapid fire and the turpentine balls and hand grenades began to work and the *Chicora* and Sullivan's Island and Fort Johnson swept the approaches with grape and shell, some of which took the liberty of bursting in the fort and the jig was up. They had come ashore expecting to find easy access through the broken arches, all of which are filled with sand. Their boats were broken by grenades and masses of masonry and bricks and our muskets would keep popping them over and in pairs and squads they quietly walked around and surrendered. To their perfect amazement. In fact they were so perfectly astonished at meeting such a reverse and so delighted at not being shot that they were quite jolly at first but by breakfast time they seemed to realize their position more fully. My dear child, twelve first rate officers and about one hundred and fifteen or twenty splendid men bagged by 70 men which was the whole force actively engaged. . . .Not the least satisfactory part of it is that not one of my men was touched.[28]

Unlike the previous operations, the Fort Sumter assault did not have the requisite ingredients for victory. There was no secrecy, as the Confederates knew it was coming and enjoyed the opportunity to ready themselves. While the strike possessed some level of celerity, coming as it did just one day after the fall of Morris Island, any benefits stemming from its swift delivery were negated by the lack of secrecy. In addition, the lack of proper planning and joint service cooperation greatly handicapped the attack and, because of the poor planning and missing coordination, the attack was not audacious, although obviously foolhardy.

The three landings discussed in this article help demonstrate the basic requirements needed to conduct a successful amphibious operation. When these requirements were met, victory was usually assured. The best example was the July 10, 1863, assault on Morris Island. The Northerners followed a well designed plan that detailed the roles of each service and defined the obligation of each commander. Tactical secrecy was kept and the attack was carried out in a swift and bold manner. Victory followed.

All of these elements were also present at the Battle of Port Royal Sound. Even though Du Pont kept full control of the operation and made all the plans, the attack was bold and achieved tactical surprise by its ability to so easily overpower the Confederate defenders. Of course there was no amphibious landing since Du Pont wanted to keep the attack a naval affair; however, had the Union forces been landed and moved inland they could have trapped the Southerners on Hilton Head and captured not only Fort Walker but also its garrison. On the other hand, the Fort Sumter assault clearly demonstrates what happens to an amphibious landing when there is no joint service cooperation or secrecy, either tactical or strategic, and when audacity becomes recklessness.

In the Civil War (as it is today), the watch words for amphibious operations were: surprise your enemy, move swiftly, be bold and forceful and have a set system of command. Without these attributes, the consequences of an amphibious landing will mirror the disastrous attack on Fort Sumter and allow the defenders to write something similar to what Major Elliott wrote after his successful defense of Fort Sumter:

> I do not know how many got off or how large the attacking party was but I had things well in hand to have thrashed three times the number we did defeat.[29]

Notes

1. Egbert L. Viele, "The Port Royal Expedition, 1861: The First Union Victory of the Civil War," *Magazine of American History*, XIV, (October, 1885), pp. 329-340.

2. Ibid., pp. 329-334; Daniel Ammen, "Du Pont and the Port Royal Expedition," in *Battles and Leaders of the Civil War*, 4 Vols., (New York: Thomas Yoseloff, 1956), vol. 1, pp. 671-673; John D. Hayes, ed., *Samuel Francis Du Pont: A Selection from his Civil War Letters*, 3 Vols., (Ithaca, New York: Cornell University Press, 1969), p. 171; *Official Records of the Union and Confederate Navies in the War of the Rebellion*, 31 Vols., (Washington D.C.: Government Printing Office, 1901), Ser. I, Vol. 12, pp. 214-215, hereinafter cited as *ORN*. All references are to Series I unless otherwise noted.

3. Ammen, "Du Pont and Port Royal," pp. 674, 691, Viele, "Port Royal Expedition," pp. 329-331;

4. Hayes, *Du Pont*, p. 181.

5. *ORN* 12, pp. 214-215; Hayes, *Du Pont*, pp. 171, 179, 181.

6. Viele, "Port Royal Expedition," pp. 333-336; Ammen, "Du Pont and Port Royal," pp. 674-677; *ORN* 12, pp. 259-261; *The War of the Rebellion: A Compilation of the Official Records of the Union and Confederate Armies*, 128 Vols., (Washington, D.C.:

Government Printing Office, 1882), Series I, Vol. 6, pp. 6-27, hereinafter cited as *OR*. All references are to Series I unless otherwise noted.

7. Hayes, *Du Pont*, pp. 181, 201, 217-219; *ORN* 12, p. 228; *OR* 6, pp. 3-6.

8. Hayes, *Du Pont*, pp. 224-225; *OR* 6, pp. 3-4.

9. Gideon Welles, *Diary of Gideon Welles*, 3 Vols. (Boston: Houghton Mifflin Company, 1911) Vol. 1, pp. 312-317, 325-326, 335-337; Quincy Adams Gillmore, *Engineer and Artillery Operations Against the Defenses of Charleston Harbor in 1863* (New York: Nostrand, 1865), pp. 12-22; Madeleine V. Dahlgren, *Memoirs of John H. Dahlgren* (Boston: Osgood, 1882), pp. 392-395, 525-526.

10. *ORN* 14, p. 446; 28, pt. 1, pp. 350-351, 414; George Stoddard, "The 100th Regiment on Folly Island," *Niagara Frontier*, I (1954), pp. 78-80; Charles K. Caldwell, *The Old Sixth Regiment: Its War Record* (New Haven: Tuttle, Morehouse and Taylor, 1875), p. 64; Luther S. Dickey, *History of the Eighty-fifth Regiment Pennsylvania Volunteer Infantry* (New York: J. C. Powers, 1915), pp. 256-258; Charles Inglesby, *Historic Sketch of the First Regiment of South Carolina Artillery (Regulars)* (Charleston: Walker, Evans and Cogswell, 1890), p. 10.

11. *OR* 28, pt. 1, p. 10; Dahlgren, *Memoirs*, pp. 397-400; James Toutelloutte, *A History of Company K of the Seventh Connecticut Volunteer Infantry in the Civil War* (n.p., 1910), pp. 107-108.

12. *ORN* 14, pp. 220, 314, 327; George E. Belknap, "Reminiscences of the Siege of Charleston," *Military Historical Society of Massachusetts Papers*, Vol. 12, pp. 175-176.

13. *ORN* 14, p. 327; Toutelloutte, *History of Company K*, pp. 107-108.

14. Ibid., p. 108; Daniel Eldridge, *Third New Hampshire Regiment* (Boston: E. B. Stillings, 1893), p. 300, C. Jacobi, *Gezogenen Geschuetzo der Amerikaner bei der Belagerunng Von Charleston* (*The Rifled Batteries of the Americans at the Siege of Charleston*), translated by A. Beehler (Berlin: Strikker, 1886), pp. 7-10.

15. Eldridge J. Copp, *Reminiscences of the War of the Rebellion* (Nashua: Telegraph Publishing Company, 1911), pp. 225-227; Caldwell, *The Old Sixth Regiment*, p. 66; Henry F. Little, *The Seventh Regiment* (Concord: J. Evan, 1896), pp. 107-108; Toutelloutte, *History of Company K*, p. 108; Gillmore, *Engineer and Artillery Operations*, p. 28; Stryker, "Three Days in the Civil War," William R. Perkins Library, Duke University, Durham, North Carolina, p. 21.

16. *OR* 28, pt. 1, p. 354; Eldridge, *Third New Hampshire*, pp. 300-302.

17. *Charleston Courier*, July 16, 1863; *Richmond Despatch*, July 14, 1863; William Lawrence Haskins, *The History of the First Regiment of Artillery* (Portland: Thurston, 1879), p. 178; John Johnson, *The Defense of Charleston Harbor* (Charleston: Walker, Evans, Cogswell, 1890), p. 90.

18. *ORN* 14, pp. 317, 320, 325-326, 329-330; Dahlgren, *Memoirs*, p. 398.

19. *ORN* 14, p. 329; Little, *Seventh Regiment*, pp. 107-109.

20. Caldwell, *Sixth Regiment*, p. 111; Little, *Seventh Regiment*, p. 108; Copp, *Reminiscences of the War*, pp. 227-228; Johnson, *Defense of Charleston Harbor*, p. 90; Eldridge, *Third New Hampshire*, pp. 301-302; *OR* 28, pt. 1, pp. 354-361; *Charleston Mercury*, July 17, 1863; Toutelloutte, *History of Company K*, 154.

21. *OR* 28, pt. 1, pp. 354-355, 413-414; Toutelloutte, *History of Company K*, pp. 111-113; Copp, *Reminiscences of War*, p. 229; Belknap, "The Siege of Charleston," p. 176; Caldwell, *Sixth Regiment*, p. 67; W. W. H. Davis, *History of the 104th Pennsylvania* (Philadelphia: Rodgers, 1886), pp. 245-246; Eldridge, *Third New Hampshire*, p. 302; Johnson, *Defense of Charleston Harbor*, p. 90.

22. Robert C. Gilchrist, "Confederate Defense of Morris Island," *Charleston Yearbook*, (Charleston: News and Courier Press, 1884), p. 361; Johnson Hagood, *Memoirs of the War of Secession* (Columbia: The State Company, 1910), p. 136; Johnson, *Defense of Charleston*, p. 90; *OR* 28, pt. 1, p. 414; *Charleston Mercury*, July 13, 1863; Caldwell, *Old Sixth Regiment*, p. 68; Copp, *Reminiscences of War*, pp. 230-234; Little, *Seventh Regiment*, pp. 109-113; Toutellette, *History of Company K*, pp. 112, 163, 173; Eldridge, *Third New Hampshire*, pp. 303-304; Stryker, "Three Days in the Civil War," pp. 22-26.

23. Little, *Seventh Regiment*, pp. 109-110; Johnson, *Defense of Charleston*, p. 90; Davis, *History of the 104th Pennsylvania*, p. 246; *OR* 28, pt. 1, pp. 2-38, 210-212, 356-361, 414.

24. Ibid., pp. 1-38, pt. 2, pp. 21-22; Alfred P. Rockwell, "The Operations against Charleston," *Military Historical Society of Massachusetts Papers*, 9, p. 74; George Henry Gordon, *A War Diary of Events in the War of the Great Rebellion: 1863-1865* (Boston: Osgood, 1882), pp. 195-196.

25. *ORN* 14, pp. 566-579, 606-608; Gordon, *War Diary*, pp. 202, 216.

26. *ORN* 14, pp. 608-609.

27. Ibid., pp. 606-640; *OR* 28, pt. 2, p. 89; Alfred S. Roe, *The Twenty-fourth Regiment Massachusetts Volunteers 1861-1866: New England Guard Regiment* (Worcester, Twenty-fourth Veteran Association, 1907), pp. 222-233.

28. Letter of Stephen Elliott, September 11, 1863, Fran Williamson Collection, Parris Island Museum, Parris Island, South Carolina; *ORN* 14, pp. 606-640.

29. Ibid.

General Edward Wild's African Brigade in the Siege of Charleston, South Carolina

Steven D. Smith

T he call to arms had come from black ministers and leaders whose recruitment posters admonished them, "Fail Now and Our Race is Doomed on this the soil of our birth."[1] And so free black men came from such homes as Yarmouth, Nova Scotia, Pickaway, Ohio, Memphis, Indiana, and Providence, Rhode Island, to sign up with the 55th Massachusetts Regiment at Readville, Massachusetts. There they trained to be Union soldiers in the spring and summer of 1863, and then were shipped to New Bern, North Carolina, where they met men of the same color, but of a very different culture. The new men, who had been free for only months or in some cases, days, were now members of the 1st North Carolina Colored Infantry. Together, the two regiments trained at New Bern as Brig. Gen. Edward A. Wild's 'African Brigade,' but soon traveled south to Folly Island, South Carolina, where they engaged in the arduous task of siege warfare against Confederate forces in and around Charleston.

Not all survived. While a few died in the clamor and terror of battle, the vast majority died lonely, singular, fever deaths—lost to their families, their friends and their race until May 11, 1987. On that day the South Carolina Institute of Archaeology and Anthropology received a call from a relic collector. The collector and a friend had found human bones at what was once a Civil War campsite. The bones had been exposed when workers cut a road through a small forested area being developed for housing at the edge of the town of Folly

Beach, South Carolina. Would someone recover these bones before they were lost to development?

As Deputy State Archaeologist for South Carolina at that time I had received many such telephone calls over the past three years. Sometimes the bones discovered turned out to be cow or deer bones, or not even bones at all. Worse, sometimes this kind of call led to the discovery of real human remains. If so, the agonizing process of trying to do everything necessary with but limited time and funding began. Something had to be done, and I arranged to meet the collectors at the site. Thus began a two-year project involving three separate archaeological excavations, a continual process of analysis of the sites and human bones, intensive archival investigations, and eventual reburial of the human remains.

This is the story of the 55th Massachusetts Volunteer Infantry and the 1st North Carolina, known collectively in 1863 as Wild's African Brigade. The focus of the essay is their participation in the campaign to take Charleston. It is also the story of the rediscovery of at least eighteen soldiers of Wild's Brigade, who died while stationed on Folly Island, their excavation by archaeologists and their eventual reburial in Beaufort National Cemetery, South Carolina. It is just one example out of thousands of examples of Americans who gave their most cherished possession—their own lives—for freedom.

The Siege of Charleston: An Overview

> What astonishes us here, is that you folks in the North should continue to imagine that we are going to capture Charleston. We have no such ridiculous aspirations. We are content to live on sand hills, eat salt junk and drink dirty water. It is true that the [New York] *Herald* startles us sometimes by showing some trifling advantages we have unwittingly gained; but I assure you, my dear fellow, that we don't intend to do anything energetic or dashing, and that such little episodes are purely accidental.[2]

So wrote Sergeant Wightman sarcastically in a letter home while sweltering on the beaches of Folly Island. He and some 12,000 other Union soldiers were participating in what would be the longest siege of the American Civil War: the siege of Charleston. Eventually, in February of 1865, Charleston would fall to the Union, but by then other events of war would render the city militarily unimportant. But during that hot, muggy August, discouraged by the insects, heat and lack of progress, Wightmam was probably accurately expressing the attitude of most of his comrades. Many were questioning what had brought them to a small, mosquito-infested barrier island in South Carolina.

What brought them to Folly Island was the strategic interest of Charleston. Through much of the Civil War the city was of critical importance to both the North and South. Without major industrial strength of its own, the South had to rely on European and other nations for rifles, swords, cannon, medicines, and even food. Ports like Wilmington, Savannah, and New Orleans were important distribution points where materials arrived from overseas and were shipped to Confederate armies throughout the South. At that time Charleston was probably the most important seaport on the South Atlantic coast. From her protected harbor a railroad network ran north to North Carolina and Virginia, and south to Georgia. Some sixty-three steam blockade runners operated in and out of this port of call. Charleston, "That viper's nest and breeding place of rebellion," as one Federal referred to it, was as crucial to Southern morale to hold as it was to Northern morale to take. The capture of Charleston would be a "deathblow" to the rebellion, according to Thomas Dudley, the United States consul at Liverpool.[3]

But Charleston refused to fall. It was well protected from naval attack, both by natural features and by man-made fortifications built long before the war. Central to its defenses was Fort Sumter, sitting formidably on the south side of the main channel. Castle Pickney on Shutes Island and Fort Moultrie on Sullivans Island completed the ring of brick forts defending the city. Confederate General P. G. T. Beauregard added to these key fortresses a series of earthen batteries around the perimeter of the harbor. These batteries included additional works at Fort Moultrie, as well as Battery Beauregard on Sullivans Island, Fort Johnson on James Island, and Batteries Wagner and Gregg on Morris Island.

Protecting Charleston from a land attack was more problematic. Without adequate troops, Maj. Gen. John C. Pemberton, who replaced Beauregard, could not cover all possible invasion scenarios. Instead, he concentrated on protecting Charleston from James Island, the most likely route of attack, and left the outer islands like Edisto, John's, Folly and Coles islands uncontested. On James Island he built an extensive line of earthworks and awaited the arrival of the Union forces.

President Abraham Lincoln quickly recognized the importance of denying the Confederacy access to Europe's markets and as early as April 1861, had ordered a blockade of Southern ports. Later that year the Federal Navy occupied Port Royal, South Carolina, while the army landed at Hilton Head, thus establishing a base for operations in the southern Atlantic. Soldiers, sailors and supplies crowded into these bases and prepared for the capture of Charleston. The campaign began on December 20, 1861, with hardly an auspicious begin-

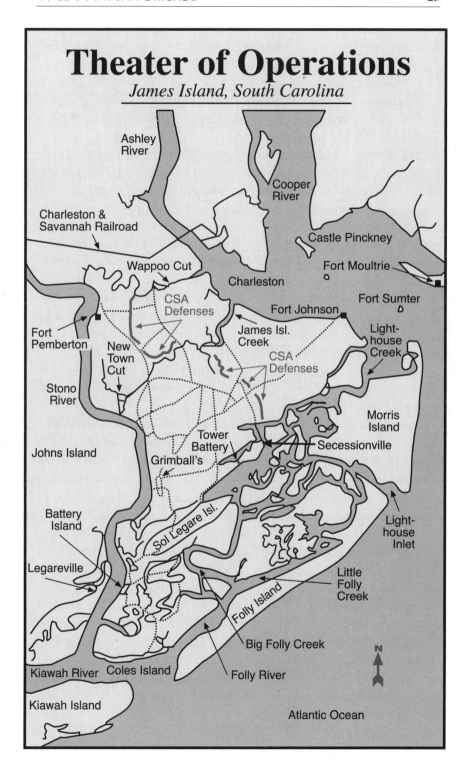

Theater of Operations
James Island, South Carolina

Ashley River

Cooper River

Charleston & Savannah Railroad

Wappoo Cut

Castle Pinckney

Charleston

Fort Moultrie

CSA Defenses

Fort Johnson

Fort Sumter

Fort Pemberton

New Town Cut

James Isl. Creek

Light-house Creek

CSA Defenses

Stono River

Morris Island

Johns Island

Tower Battery

Grimball's

Secessionville

Battery Island

Sol Legare Isl.

Light-house Inlet

Legareville

Little Folly Creek

Folly Island

Big Folly Creek

Kiawah River   Coles Island

Folly River

N

Kiawah Island

Atlantic Ocean

ning. The Union Navy sunk a number of otherwise useless old whaling ships and merchantmen in the main harbor channel in an attempt to block off entry. This action, and a similar attempt a month later, did little to block the harbor. The wrecks were sunk in place with stone, and once the wooden hulks gave way, the current rushing against the stone scoured the channel. The North had unintentionally improved the channel's navigation.

Badly in need of a victory to strengthen Northern war resolve, Lincoln demanded further action. It came in the form of Col. (nominated Brig. General) Henry W. Benham, who led a 7,500 man force up the Stono River and landed on James Island on June 2, 1862. Benham skirmished with the Confederates but failed to attack in force. It was General David Hunter, commander of the Department of the South, who apparently held Benham back, awaiting reinforcements. Unimpressed by the Union challenge, the Confederates took the initiative and attacked first on June 10. This small unsuccessful thrust was repulsed and accomplished little except to encourage the North that victory would be easy. Less than one week later on June 16, Benham rammed portions of his army against a strong Confederate earthwork at Secessionville in what he eventually called a "reconnaissance in force."[4]

In a furious three and one half hour battle the Federals suffered 683 casualties, their opponents, 204. One Confederate who toured the battlefield afterward wrote his mother "such a sight I do not wish to see again. I saw men laying in all kinds of postures, some in the very act of shooting off their Guns, some loading & some looked as though they were praying after they were wounded & died."[5] Secessionville was a bloody failure for Union arms and not the "action" Lincoln was seeking.

For the next ten months Union leaders bickered over strategy. Assistant Secretary of the Navy, Gustavus V. Fox, ordered Adm. Samuel F. Du Pont to run his squadron of ironclads into Charleston Harbor past the ring of Confederate fortifications. Du Pont, recognizing the madness of such an unsupported move, delayed rather than implement the plan forthwith. Fox finally agreed to support the naval attack with a simultaneous landing of troops on Morris Island, and for a short while, a massive land and sea attack was being planned. The idea was that during the ironclad attack troops would conduct an amphibious landing on Morris Island and take Confederate Battery Wagner. Then, siege guns would be emplaced to finish the job of neutralizing Fort Sumter. Without Fort Sumter, so the theory went, Charleston would fall. But the plan fell apart when both the army and navy lost heart in their respective abilities to get troops en masse onto Morris Island.

Eventually, a joint—though less bold—move was approved. On April 6 and 7, 1863, Col. Joshua B. Howell's XVIII Army Corps, together with portions of Brig. Gen. Alfred Terry's X Army corps, some 10,000 soldiers altogether, landed on Folly Island.[6] They immediately marched to the northern end of Folly in preparation for an assault against Morris Island planned for the following day after the naval attack by Du Pont. Despite feeble attempts at concealment, Confederate pickets watched the entire affair. They were well prepared for the Union's next move.

Du Pont, unconvinced that a naval assault into Charleston Harbor would work, quickly fulfilled his own prophecy. In less than two hours the assault was over. From protected positions, with guns ranged and sighted, the Confederate cannon registered 520 hits against Du Pont's hesitantly attacking fleet, severely damaging five of his seven ironclads. The Union navy got off only 139 shots against at least 15 times the Confederate fire. In a masterful bit of understatement, Du Pont wrote "I have attempted to take the bull by the horns, but he was too much for us."[7] With the defeat of the ironclads, the Union infantry on Folly Island was left to dig in, hold on and await further orders.

They were left waiting until July, when orders for offensive action finally arrived. By that time the soldiers on Folly Island were under a different command. Brigadier General Israel Vogdes [pronounced vog-days] was placed in command of the troops building defensive positions on Folly Island, while Maj. Gen. Quincy A. Gillmore was placed in command of the Department of the South. Union troops continued to land on Folly, Coles and North Edisto islands.

Gillmore's strategy for the capture of Charleston was similar to previous proposals. Specifically, the infantry would cross over to Morris Island in force, supported by masked batteries on the northern end of Folly Island. To keep the Confederates guessing, a detachment of troops would feint an attack on James Island at the same time. Once on Morris, they would immediately move northeast along the beach to capture Battery Wagner, and from there begin the process of silencing Fort Sumter through bombardment.

Preparations for the attack concentrated on the northern end of Folly Island. Working at night in total silence, their "duty was quite arduous," wrote one Connecticut soldier.[8] Gillmore attempted to conceal more than 11,000 soldiers and ten batteries, 47 field rifles and mortars, each with 200 rounds of ammunition. Such a large force was hardly invisible. Throughout the preparations Confederates watched the activities while pickets taunted the Unionists that "General Beauregard had such an exalted opinion of the Yankees on Folly Island that he was coming over. . . .[to give them] all a 'farm six feet by two.'"[9]

Even though all evidence pointed to an imminent assault on Morris Island, Beauregard was still worried that the main assault against Charleston would be through his lines on James Island. Given that possibility, he could not afford to move too many troops from James Island into his fortifications on Morris Island. There was little he could do but wait while his soldiers taunted the Federals.

The assault was finally attempted on July 8, 1863. It began with Brig. Gen. Alfred H. Terry's feint onto James Island with 3,800 men. A landing in force on Morris Island was to follow Terry's demonstration, but the weather did not cooperate and the main attack was not launched until July 10. After a two-hour bombardment by the artillery on Folly Island, supported by gunboats in the Atlantic, the amphibious landing was not strongly challenged. The Union forces pushed through the Confederate fortifications on the southern end of Morris Island and proceeded up the beach toward Battery Wagner.

The battle for Wagner is well documented.[10] The Federals attacked the next day and were repulsed after heavy casualties. A week later on July 18, the 54th Massachusetts Colored Regiment, the first black regiment from a Northern state, was severely blooded in another frontal attack against the battery. Over forty percent of the regiment was lost, many buried by the Southerners along with their commander, Col. Robert Shaw. The *New York Tribune* reported that the 54th "made Fort Wagner such a name for the colored race as Bunker Hill has been for ninety years to the white Yankees."[11]

With the loss of more than 1,500 men in two attacks against Battery Wagner, in addition to the losses at Secessionville, the offensive spirit of the Union understandably waned. A long siege began that was to last nineteen months. During the siege, Charleston and Fort Sumter were subjected to sporadic bombardments while the Confederate defenders returned fire. In September the Confederates abandoned Battery Wagner after the Union army had spent months zigzagging trenches closer and closer to the bastion. For the Confederates, Battery Wagner had fulfilled its mission well, costing the Union much time, effort and blood. Throughout the rest of 1863 and 1864, the Union maintained soldiers on Folly, Morris, and Coles islands and would occasionally probe the Rebel lines on James Island. Artillery duels and bombardments were traded back and forth. Meanwhile the events of war elsewhere in the South continued to make Charleston less and less important to the final outcome of the war.

During the winter of 1864, the Union high command began reducing the number of units besieging Charleston until there was only enough men to man the guns and to occasionally skirmish with the Confederates. Eventually, the

forces of Maj. Gen. William T. Sherman threatened Charleston from the rear, and
on February 17, 1865, the siege ended when the Confederates abandoned the city
and the coast to the North. By then, Charleston was not the prize so desperately
needed in 1862. Less than two months later, Robert E. Lee surrendered his army
to U.S. Grant.

A History of Edward Wild's Brigade

Among the 12,000 or so Union soldiers who would take part in the siege of
Charleston were nine regiments composed solely of black troops. With Abraham
Lincoln's initial call for 75,000 volunteers at the beginning of the war, blacks in
the Northern states immediately attempted to enlist but were promptly rejected.[12]
The reasons given for rejecting black participation were numerous. At first, the
war was a war to preserve the Union, and the slavery question was an issue that
many white Northerners wanted to avoid. Lincoln feared that arming the black
man would drive the border states into the Confederacy. Manpower was not a
problem since white volunteers were flooding recruiting stations across the country. Many of these whites considered blacks inferior and were convinced that they
would not stand in battle. According to the prevailing prejudice, the years spent
in slavery had made the black unfit for military duty.

Meanwhile, abolitionists and free blacks loudly proclaimed the right to fight
for the freedom of those in bondage. The most famous and ardent supporter of
this cause was Frederick Douglas, who hoped that participation in the military
would bring about equality of rights during peacetime. His often repeated quote
from an 1863 speech in Philadelphia spoke to the heart of the issue:

> Once let the black man get upon his person the brass letters U.S.; let him get an
> eagle on his button, and a musket on his shoulder, and the bullets in his pocket,
> and there is no power on the earth or under the earth which can deny that he
> has earned the right of citizenship in the United States.[13]

While the debate over black participation raged, casualties rose in the Union
armies. As the martial spirit of the volunteers waned, the ranks began to thin.
Eventually, the war's objectives grew to include emancipation, and Northerners
began to question why the black man could not shed his blood as well. When
Lincoln issued the Emancipation Proclamation in January of 1863, the door was
open for abolitionists to press for official use of black soldiers. One ardent
abolitionist, John Albion Andrew, was in a perfect position take immediate action

after the proclamation. Andrew, the governor of Massachusetts, saw his continued work for black participation rewarded on January 26, 1863, with the authorization to raise a regiment of black volunteers. His recruitment efforts throughout the Northern states raised two regiments of free blacks, the 54th and 55th Massachusetts Volunteer Infantry.

The 55th Massachusetts mustered in at Readville, Massachusetts on May 12, 1863, and when the 54th Massachusetts left for Hilton Head Island, South Carolina, the 55th immediately took over their abandoned barracks to learn the art of soldiering. Lieutenant Colonel N. P. Hallowell and Capt. A. S. Hartwell, both formerly with the 54th Massachusetts, commanded the cadre that would train the recruits pouring in from across the northern states.[14]

The men of the 55th Massachusetts were among thousands of free blacks living in the North prior to the war. Their recorded birthplaces included: Pennsylvania with 139, Ohio with 222, Indiana with 97, Kentucky with 68, and Missouri with 66. Other states providing large numbers of recruits were Illinois with 56 and New York with 23. Only 22 men were born in Massachusetts. Some 247 of the 55th had at one time been slaves and of those, 106 were from Virginia, 30 from North Carolina, and 24 from Tennessee. There were three men from Canada, and one was born in Africa.[15]

Except for their color, the men of the 55th Massachusetts represented a typical cross-section of white Americans in the mid-nineteenth century. The vast majority, 596, were farmers, and 76 were common laborers. There were 34 barbers, 50 waiters, 27 cooks and 21 blacksmiths within the 55th's ranks. Twenty-seven others were teamsters and an additional 20 were sailors. Among the more interesting occupations were six teachers, three engineers, a confectioner, clergyman, and a student. Many were educated: 477 could read and 319 could read and write. During their training at Readville and on Folly Island, many others took the opportunity to learn to read and write. They averaged 23 1/4 years of age and five feet seven inches in height.[16]

Training practices at Readville, Massachusetts, had a remarkable similarity to modern basic training. The men drilled in squads, companies and battalions. Battalion drill occurred every evening except when four or six mile road marches were scheduled. The men performed guard duty and were subjected to the mundane duties of policing the grounds and inspecting the barracks. The recruits were also used for fatigue duty at Camp Meigs. Most of the men survived basic training and with typical unit pride, their regimental history states:

This photograph of the officers of the 55th Massachusetts was taken in Readville, Massachusetts (date unknown). From left to right: Dr. William Symington Brown; Lt. Col. Alfred Stedman Hartwell; 1st Lt. & Adjutant William Penrose Hallowell; Col. Norwood Penrose Hallowell; Dr. Burt Greene Wilder; Dr. Asst. Surgeon; Maj. Charles Bernard Fox; and Capt. Sigorney Wales. The original is in the possession of Mary Hartwell Truesdell, Bath, Maine. Thanks also to Kathy Dhalle, Rome, NY.

No regiment left Massachusetts with a better outfit than the fifty-fifth. Few, if any, in better drill and discipline for the length of time they had under instruction; none with more faithful, intelligent, and efficient corps of officers, or men more thoroughly devoted to the cause which they had undertaken.[17]

With the world watching regimental pride did indeed run deep. At the end of the tattoo roll-call on the first evening:

One of their number stepped from the ranks and made a simple and appropriate prayer, and the whole squad joined in singing one of their peculiar hymns. The practice thus commenced was continued, and adopted by each company in succession.[18]

Armed with Enfield rifles and Springfield muskets, the 55th Massachusetts broke camp for the war on July 21, 1863, embarking from Boston on the steamer *Cahawba*. The regiment arrived at New Bern, North Carolina, four days later on July 25, where together with the 1st North Carolina Colored Infantry, it was assigned to Brig. Gen. Edward A. Wild's "African Brigade."

In bold contrast to the 55th Massachusetts, the men of the 1st North Carolina had been slaves only a few months before they became soldiers. General Wild, assisted by Joseph E. Williams, a well known black abolitionist, recruited from among those slaves seeking safety and freedom behind Union lines. They also sought out recruits in raids across the North Carolina countryside. In one particular raid:

we were informed that there were upwards of thirty colored prisoners in the Duplin Court House that were to be tried for their lives for attempting to escape inside the lines of the United State forces. We tried to break down the door with axes. . .This door seemed to be about as hard as

Brig. Gen. Edward A. Wild

Generals in Blue

that of any iron safe. Finally the key was sent for, threatening the sheriff with vengeance in case of refusal, in the form of tar and feathers. . . .[The door is opened] The thirty was a fabulous number, which had diminished to three live colored men; their lives were saved. Two of them came on to Newbern to join Wild's brigade.[19]

General Wild set up a camp for the slaves and their families on Roanoke Island, North Carolina. At New Bern, Wild and their commander, Col. James C. Beecher, formed and trained the regiment. Schools were also established. While in training, a group of black women ordered a battle flag for the unit. "The flag is to be made of blue silk, with a yellow silk fringe around the border. On one side the Goddess of Liberty is represented with her right foot resting on a copperhead snake. On the reverse side, a large gilt rising sun with the word 'Liberty' in very large letters over the sun."[20] Demonstrating a close tie to Massachusetts, the flag was consecrated by Governor Andrew.

Only five days after the arrival of the Massachusetts troops in North Carolina, the 55th Massachusetts and 1st North Carolina sailed for Folly Island, landing on August 3rd, and:

proceeded along the beach to the extreme northerly end of Folly Island, and bivouacked in the sand. So urgent was the call for men that heavy details for fatigue were made at once, and it was not until after five days that the camp vacated by the forty-seventh New York, about four hundred yards south of Light-house inlet, in a small grove of palmetto on the beach, was assigned to the Fifty-fifth, the First North Carolina going into camp directly north of them.[21]

From that time on, Wild's Brigade was engaged in the heavy labor of preparing positions on Folly and Morris Islands.

One rationale for sending the 55th Massachusetts to South Carolina was the mistaken and stereotypical belief that the black man could better stand the hot, humid weather of the South. The men of the 55th, however, almost immediately suffered under the southern sun, with sickness and diseases thinning the ranks. In the first seven weeks on Folly Island, 12 men were lost, and by the end of December the toll had reached 23. Exacerbating the situation, the 55th Massachusetts worked and slept in the open. Having left New Bern hurriedly without tents, knapsacks, blankets or personal gear. The missing accouterments did not arrive until September, but by that time much of it had been stolen or destroyed.[22]

A photograph depicting an unidentified Federal camp in the interior of Folly Island. This location strongly resembles one described (and depicted in a hand-drawn map) by Major Fox. *USAMHI.*

The heavy labor continued through the fall. During this time, detachments of the 55th Massachusetts and 1st North Carolina worked on many of the adjacent islands, assisting in the various labor parties hauling cannon, building gun emplacements and standing guard. Only rarely did they have a chance to engage the enemy. Once, while on the north end of the island, a small detachment of the 1st North Carolina was sent out on a patrol reminiscent of future excursions that would be conducted during World War II or Vietnam. On January 1, 1864, Lieutenant Remick turned in the following report:

> I have the honor to report that in accordance with orders from the Major Commanding I proceeded on the evening of the 31st of December with twelve men and one sergent [sic] to Pawnee Landing. There I took a boat and pulled quietly down Folly River until I arrived at a large creek opposite pickett Post No. 2-3rd Brigade. I ascended this creek until I came to a creek turning off to the right which creek I followed up for the distance of two hundred and fifty to three hundred yards—I then pulled in shore; made my boat fast to the long grass and lay in wait for boat or boats of the enemy. After laying there until between three and four this morning and seeing no signs of any boat I returned to camp.[23]

In November of 1863, most of the brigade moved inland to the back of the island along Folly River. By this time morale had improved somewhat and the weather was turning more healthful, although casualties to disease still occurred. The brigade remained on Folly until February 13 and 14, 1864. By that time events elsewhere demanded their presence in Florida, and the two regiments left the Charleston area without firing a shot at the enemy.

In Florida, the 55th and 1st North Carolina (now redesignated the 35th USCI) actively campaigned against the Confederates. The 35th USCI saw their first combat in the Battle of Olustee, where the Union army was mauled on February 20, 1864. The 35th, 8th and 54th Massachusetts joined six white regiments in the hard fight, losing 1,861 men. Of those, 230 of the 35th were killed, wounded or missing.[24] After Olustee, Wild's Brigade was disbanded while still in Florida. After the Jacksonville Campaign, the two regiments served under different commands, although they would meet again at the Battle of Honey Hill. The 35th USCI went on to distinguish itself throughout the balance of the war, seeing action at Black Creek, Florida, and in South Carolina at St. John's River and Honey Hill, accumulating 53 combat deaths during those engagements.[25]

The 55th Massachusetts returned to Folly Island in mid-April 1864, hardened campaigners but still untested in combat. The scene around Charleston had changed considerably since their departure. The 55th found the island almost deserted, with units detached and scattered over the many small islands in the area. The 55th Massachusetts was also broken into small detachments, to perform fatigue details and guard duty throughout the barrier islands.

Eventually war found the 55th Massachusetts. On May 21 the Bay Staters, along with the 103rd New York, skirmished with Confederates on James Island. Nineteen-year-old Private Phineas Cost [or Corst], Company E of Rockaway, New York, became the first of the 55th to receive a combat wound, a musket ball in the leg.[26] Two days later the entire regiment made a feint on Johns Island. Neither engagement was significant or particularly bloody, but both gave the men of the 55th some combat experience, thereby improving morale.

Throughout the summer of 1864 both the Confederates and the Federals continued to withdraw men from the Charleston area. In June, the Unionists believed that the Confederates were so weak that they could again attempt a thrust against the city. On the first of July, Brig. Gen. Alexander Schimmelfennig led yet another attack against the James Island lines. Just as Benham had in June 1862, Schimmelfennig chose to strike Fort Lamar in Secessionville. The 55th Massachusetts was placed in the center reserve of the battle line, and it looked as if they would it would miss combat yet again. But when the center of the Union line was checked by a blast of musket and canister fire, the 55th Massachusetts immediately deployed and charged the Confederate battery, capturing two twelve-pound Napoleons.[27]

One sergeant of the 55th Massachusetts wrote proudly of their performance:

> Could you have been on the battle-field on the morning of July 1st, and seen them under a shower of shot and shell deploy into line of battle when it seemed as though the day was lost by the giving way of two regiments (one white, and the other colored, both rushing back discomforted)–I say, could you have seen the old 55th rush in, with the shout of 'Remember Fort Pillow!" you would have thought that nothing human could have withstood their impetuosity. We know no defeat. The guns we were bent on having.[28]

The guns were kept by the 55th for future use against their former owners.

The engagement was not without cost. Seven men were killed and two mortally wounded, while 19 others, including two officers, were wounded. Unfortunately, while the wounded were carried back under fire the dead were left on the field. Although plans were made to recover them that evening, the 55th was ordered to fall back and the dead were left to the Confederates. Eight months later officers of the 55th Massachusetts returned to the battle site and found the grisly remains of James Davis, Lewis Peck and the five others, still moldering where they had fallen. Their skulls, however, had been taken.[29]

Though the Union attack accomplished little strategically, the performance by the 55th increased its confidence and morale. The battle on James Island proved to be only a small test; the real proof of their mettle was soon to come. On November 26, the 55th was shipped to Hilton Head, South Carolina, with five days cooked rations and 140 cartridges per man. On the evening of the 29th, the men landed at Boyd's Neck, South Carolina, and the next day joined a column of Union soldiers, including the 54th Massachusetts and 35th USCI, on the road to Grahamville, South Carolina.

A few miles down the road the Federals encountered Confederate skirmishers, which were slowly beaten back along the roadway to their "entrenchments, situated on a bluff at the further side of a small swampy creek, which crossed the main road just as it turned sharply to the left."[30] Thick woods were found on either side of the road. The bluff upon which the Southerners had constructed their works was known locally as Honey Hill.

The 55th and 54th were formed into double column and wheeled off the road into the woods on the right. The thick woods and difficult terrain, coupled with the narrow road upon which artillery and wagons were strung out, caused the units to lose their cohesion. Orders were shouted and lost in the confusion and noise of the developing battle. Still, the 54th and 55th Massachusetts and 35th USCI managed to form into battle lines and charge the bluff across a wooded swamp in a futile attempt to take the fortified position. The 55th was thrown back and twice rallied to charge again. Unable to seize the position, the exhausted soldiers were forced to admit their failure by retreating. Although far less celebrated in the popular literature, the fury and violence of the Battle of Honey Hill was on a par with what the 54th Massachusetts experienced in its rush against the ramparts of Battery Wagner. Even a Confederate account of the battle gave credit to the black soldier's aggressiveness:

> The Negroes, as usual, formed the advance, and had nearly reached the creek when our batteries opened upon them down the road with a terrible volley of special case. This threw them into temporary confusion, but the entire force, estimated at five thousand, was quickly restored to order. . . .Thus the battle raged from eleven in the morning till dark. . . .The centre and left of the enemy fought with desperate earnestness. Several attempts were made to charge our

batteries, and many got nearly across the swamp, but were in every instance forced back by the galling fire poured into them from our lines. We made a visit to the field the day following, and found the road literally strewn with their dead.[31]

On the evening of the battle the 55th and the rest of the column retreated back down the road to Boyd's Neck. The next morning's roll call "revealed a loss, in killed and wounded, of half the officers and a third of the enlisted men engaged."[32] Thirty-one soldiers from the 55th were killed and 138 were wounded.

Though most of the expedition soon left Boyd's Neck for Hilton Head, the 55th Massachusetts remained until January 1, 1865. In February the Massachusetts men once again found themselves on Folly Island where, on February 9, they formed part of a expedition to James Island. Together with the 144th and 54th New York, the 55th Massachusetts attacked Rebel positions on the island. The assault was successful at the cost of but one wounded man. Ten days later word went out that Charleston had been abandoned. The 55th entered the city on February 21, 1865:

> Few people were on the wharf when the troops landed, or in the street when the line was formed; but the streets, on the route through the city, were crowded with the colored population. Cheers, blessings, prayers, and songs were heard on every side. Men and women crowded to shake hands with the men and officers. . . .On through the streets of the rebel city passed the column, on through the chief seat of that slave power, tottering to its fall. Its walls rung to the chorus of manly voices singing 'John Brown,' 'Babylon is falling,' and the 'Battle-Cry of Freedom;' while, at intervals, the national airs, long unheard there, were played by the regimental band. The glory and triumph of this hour may be imagined, but can never be described. It was one of those occasions which happen but once in a lifetime, to be lived over in the memory for ever.[33]

The 55th Massachusetts continued to serve occupation duty through South Carolina in Monk's Corner, Eutaw Springs, Orangeburg, Summerville, Ridgeville and Mount Pleasant. On August 29, 1865, the regiment was mustered out at Mount Pleasant and formally discharged in Boston on September 23. Thirty two "commissioned officers and 822 enlisted men were mustered out; of these, 18 officers and 653 men had left Readville in 1863, and had served with the regiment from its organization."[34]

Over the course of the war the 55th Massachusetts and 35th USCI had campaigned hard and served well, proving their worth as soldiers. They had heeded the call of the recruitment posters, which cried "If we would be regarded Men, if we would forever SILENCE THE TONGUE OF CALUMNY, of prejudice and hate; let us rise NOW and fly to arms![35]

Rediscovery and Excavation

In 1865, when the Union Army finally seized Charleston, Folly Island was abandoned—devastated by its two-year intensive occupation. Throughout the island the army had camped, dug privies, wells and trash pits, constructed fortifications and buildings, raised hospital tents, cooked dinners and buried the dead. Soldiers lost buttons, buckles and ammunition, broke bottles and other personal items, threw away worn equipment and forgot where they had placed their pocket knives. All these things were left behind. Also left behind were an unknown number of their friends. Unable to be shipped home to their families, the dead were interred in numerous small regimental, brigade and division-level cemeteries.[36]

None of the soldiers could have foreseen that one day their trash and lost equipage would have value or be of interest to future generations. Certainly they could not have imagined that one hundred and twenty-four years later, archaeologists would reclaim their friends, or that scientists would return to that—in their minds, at least—very dismal little island with the purpose of learning about their experience. But that is exactly what happened in 1987.

Local and out-of-state collectors had known for decades that Folly Island was as an excellent place to find Civil War relics. Much of the modern town of Folly Beach now covers the old campgrounds, but one area remained undeveloped until the spring 1987, when construction began for a private residential community. Clearing the area turned the property from a forest with moderate to heavy understory into open, exposed sand dunes. When word of the construction activities spread, collectors swarmed in. Two avid local relic collectors discovered human bones in a road cut and eventually contacted the author.

It was clear that the cemetery was threatened by further construction of the road and probable looting by other collectors. To prevent further disturbance of the grave site, protective measures needed to be immediately implemented. A critical legal question which needed to be decided was whether the ancient cemetery could be considered an archaeological site, or whether the burials should be turned over to the Charleston County Coroner for handling as an abandoned cemetery. In 1987 South Carolina's only laws pertaining to this problem stated that persons wishing to move an abandoned cemetery must work with the local governing body to locate next of kin prior to re-interment.[37] There was no law providing for scientific examination of the remains.

The landowner and the County Coroner were contacted, along with the Charleston County Medical Examiner's Office, officials of the City of Folly Beach, the State Historic Preservation Office, and the South Carolina Coastal Council. After extensive discussion everyone agreed that the burials were not of recent origin and eventually should be reburied. They also were interested in what archaeologists could learn by excavating the site. The developer agreed to a 30-day construction delay and the author assembled a team of experts—archaeologists, physical anthropologists, and historians—to recover and study the burials.

Over the next two weeks the Institute recovered 14 burials plus a miscellaneous collection of bones found on the surface which could not be identified as from a particular individual. During sewer construction an additional four burials were recovered by another group of contract archaeologists.[38] Backhoe tests were performed around the site to be sure that no further burials were left behind (see Figure 2 on the following pages).

As modern scientists searching for understanding about past human behavior, the archaeologists arrived on site with a careful plan, or research design. This research design served to guide the excavations and direct how the archaeologists would go about each step in the process of removing the burials. The plan also outlined several important questions about the site that the archaeologists were there to answer. It was important to think of such questions beforehand so that the effort would be focused and efficient. Who were these individuals? Why were they buried on Folly Island? How had they died? Initially, the archaeologists had to confirm that the burials were Union soldiers who died during the siege of Charleston. Though the odds were very good that they were indeed deceased Federals, it was not at all certain at the outset. Complicating matters was the fact that there had been a plantation on the island, which left the possibility that the burials could be slaves. In addition, the barrier islands near Charleston had often been used to abandon the bodies of people who had died during a long transatlantic voyage. By removing the bodies from a ship before arriving in Charleston, the sailors and passengers could avoid being quarantined. Thus the Civil War was not the only possible explanation for the cemetery. The question as to general identity (i.e., Federal soldiers) was quickly

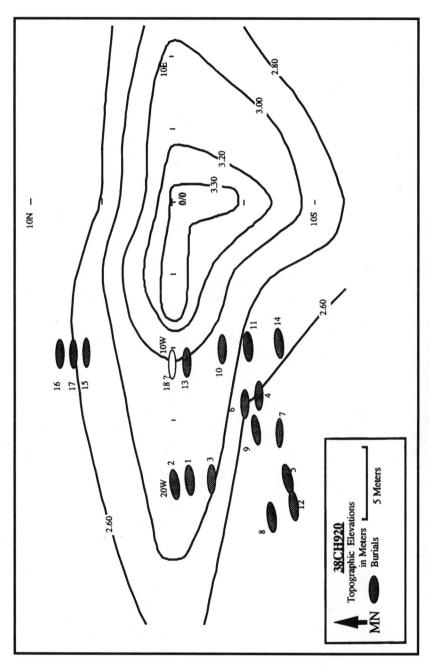

Topographic map of Wild's Brigade cemetery, site 38CH920, showing burials (SCIAA).

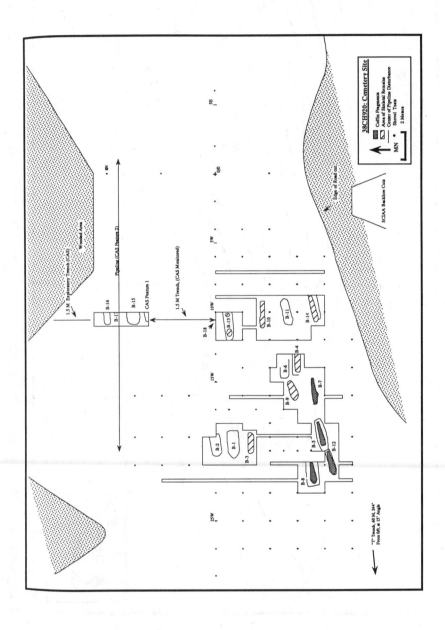

38CH920: Cemetery Site

▨ Coffin Fragments
▨ Area of Skeletal Remains
▫ Center of Pipeline Disturbance
• Shovel Tests

MN

2 Meters

answered with the recovery of the first burial, but another question soon replaced it and remained a mystery for sometime.

We recovered eighteen human burials and numerous other human bones exposed by the bulldozer. Oddly, of the eighteen human burials, only two skulls were recovered. Where were the skulls of the other sixteen? It also became readily apparent that we were not the first to uncover the graves. All but the two burials with intact skulls were disturbed to some degree or another. The disturbances clearly had nothing to do with the construction work. The corpses had been disturbed by some other cause, but what was it?

The mystery of the missing skulls and site disturbance was not solved until much more was learned about the soldiers, the site, the 55th Massachusetts and the Civil War. For the next two years we worked like detectives, piecing together the separate facts as they were gathered, analyzing these facts in light of others. The first clues came from slow, meticulous excavation of the site. By recording every observation and analyzing the results, we learned that each of the burials were dug individually to different depths. It also was discovered that the majority of the bodies had been placed in clusters rather than neat rows, although three of the graves were indeed buried in a row and at relatively the same depth, as if interred at the same time. Within each burial we observed a number of different characteristics. All but one of the soldiers were laid east/west with hands folded across their chests or abdomens, in an extended, supine position, the sole exception buried on his back or side. Although the soil did not preserve coffins particularly well, it appears that nine of the soldiers were buried in simple hexagonal caskets. We found grommets in some burials, indicating that seven of the men were wrapped in rubber blankets, including four who were also buried in coffins. Eight others must have been buried in uniform "sack coats," because the regulation number of Union uniform buttons for sack coats was found in those graves. Also discovered with the bodies were civilian buttons, indicating that some of the individuals were wearing civilian undergarments. Four men were buried with their forage caps, the buckles of which were found beside the remains. All but one of the soldiers were buried in trousers, the other either buried nude or clad in undergarments that long since had disappeared. One soldier was buried with his pipe.

While the recovered soldiers were almost all clothed in some manner, there was no evidence of shoes in any of the burials. Most of the foot bones were found in an undisturbed state, but no shoe leather or shoe nails were located. Since it is unlikely that shoe leather would have completely disintegrated, it is probable that the soldiers' shoes were removed prior to burial. Perhaps they were reused or

Burial # 5, from Site 38CH920 (see Figure 2, p. 39)
South Carolina Institute of Archaeology and Anthropology

Burial # 14, from Site 38CH920 (see Figure 2, p. 39)
South Carolina Institute of Archaeology and Anthropology

Burial # 2, from Site 38CH920 (see Figure 2, p. 39)
South Carolina Institute of Archaeology and Anthropology

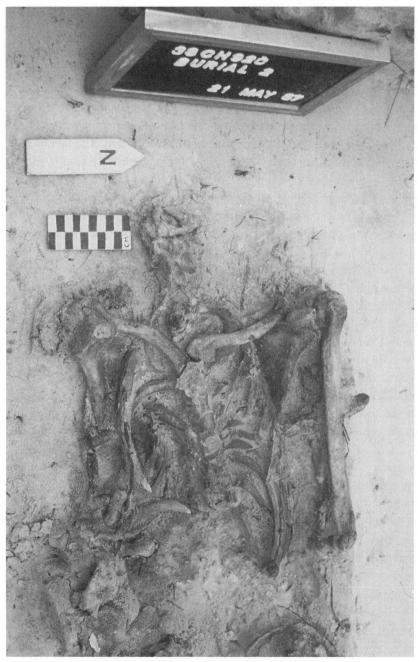

A variant image of Burial # 2, from Site 38CH920 (see Figure 2, p. 39)

South Carolina Institute of Archaeology and Anthropology

issued to new troops. The black troops on Folly Island were in great need of shoes. Colonel (then major) Fox, the 55th Massachusetts' Regimental Adjutant, once wrote that, "There are some 15 more or less in the regiment who wear No. 12 and two who wear No. 13, and it is with great difficulty we can keep them from having to go barefooted."[39]

Added to this evidence were facts learned from study of the bones. Physical anthropologists can tell archaeologists as much about human remains from the past as they can tell detectives about modern murder victims. The anthropologists were able to deduce that as a group, they were relatively healthy young black males with an average age of 25 years. They ranged in age from 16-years-old to a maximum of 40. Most of them were between 20 and 30, and only three were probably older than 30. The remains averaged five feet six inches in height (which corresponds to the average height recorded in historical documents regarding the 55th Massachusetts), and many of their bones exhibited the features of a life of heavy labor. There was no evidence of trauma to the bone as might be seen if they had died of combat wounds.[40]

The individual graves, the loosely defined rows of graves, the many different clothing characteristics noted inside each of the burials and the lack of combat wounds implied that the soldiers probably died individual deaths over an extended period. This would be consistent with the hypothesis that the soldiers died of diseases in a camp hospital. Had they all died as a result of a single incident and been buried at once, the burials would most likely have been found in neat rows at a similar depth—the expected observation resulting from of a single, organized burial detail. Or even more likely, the burial detail would have dug a trench and placed all of the dead men in a single mass grave. This is a typical method of burying men killed in combat in order to efficiently dispose of the remains. The lack of shoes also supports the theory that they died in a hospital, where their shoes would have naturally been removed at the beginning of their hospitalization, and would not have been replaced upon death.

The evidence that the burials were all black males in Union uniforms confirmed that they were members of a black Civil War military unit that had been stationed on Folly Island during the siege. But which unit? Several black regiments served on Folly Island during those years, including the legendary 54th Massachusetts. To answer this question, we turned from the ground and the remains and examined historical documents. One additional artifact from the archaeological excavations, however, gave us an important hint as to their identity. We recovered from one of the remains a sheet-brass stencil blank, which had been modified to be worn as an insignia. The blank was the number "5."

Sorting out which of the possible nine different black regiments were on Folly Island during the siege was a complex problem, exacerbated by the fact that units were constantly being detached and combined for temporary duties throughout the barrier islands. Still, the historical and archaeological evidence combined to produce a likely answer to which unit was represented among the graves. Black units on Folly Island included the following: (1) 21st United States Colored Infantry (earlier designated the 3rd and 4th South Carolina Colored Infantry); (2) 33rd USCI (1st SCCI); (3) 34th USCI (2nd SCCI); (4) 1st NCCI (North Carolina Colored Infantry, who in February 1864 became the 35th USCI); (5) Elements of the 2nd NCCI (later the 36th USCI); (6) Elements of the 3rd NCCI (who became the 37th USCI); (7) Elements of the 2nd USCI; (8) 54th Massachusetts Volunteer Regiment; and (9) 55th Massachusetts Volunteer Regiment.[41]

The service history of many of these units during the siege of Charleston quickly eliminated the 21st USCI, 34th USCI, and 54th Massachusetts. While some sources indicated that the 21st USCI served on Folly Island from April 1864 to February 1865, its members simply performed fatigue duty. The regimental camp was actually on Morris Island. On February 20, 1865, the 21st was detached from Morris Island to Charleston. The 34th USCI arrived on Folly Island on April 13, 1864, and was quickly transferred to Morris Island. The 54th Massachusetts had duty on Folly and Morris Islands from April to November 1863, but did not camp on Folly Island.[42]

Through the process of elimination, the remains had to represent members of the 2nd and 3rd NCCI, 2nd USCI, 33rd USCI, or Wild's Brigade, composed of the 1st North Carolina and 55th Massachusetts. It was known that the troops on Folly Island camped on the beaches during the summer and moved inland, to the back of the island, during the winter. From the known location of the cemetery, it was obvious that the cemetery was used primarily—possibly exclusively—during the winter months while soldiers were camped along Folly River. Which of the remaining black units camped in or near to the location of the cemetery site?

A careful analysis of the historical documents in conjunction with a contemporary and modern map of the island pinpointed the cemetery to the 1863-64 winter camp of Wild's African Brigade. As noted previously, the 55th Massachusetts and 1st North Carolina were on Folly from July 1863 to February 1864. After two months in Florida, the 55th returned to the island and remained there from April until November of 1864. The 1st North Carolina became the 35th USCI upon leaving Folly Island and did not return after the Florida campaign, although their sick remained on the island.

The published version of the 55th Massachusetts Regimental history states that in November the unit moved inland to:

> . . .a spot on the west slope of a wooded ridge, in the middle of the island, on the road leading from the Campbell House to the beach. This ridge was the third from the sea—the bluff over the beach being the first—and only a gentle rise or two of wooded ground separated it from the marshes bordering on Folly River. A good location for cold weather; it would have been decidedly unhealthy in summer, when the health of the troops could only be preserved by encamping as near as possible to the beach, exposed to the sea breeze. This camp was gradually improved, a parade ground cleared in front, and soon made, if not the best regimental camp on the island, certainly the best ever occupied there by the regiment.[43]

This location, when compared to contemporary and modern maps, corresponds exactly with the location of the cemetery. One additional piece of historical documentation indicated that the cemetery was a brigade rather than regimental cemetery, meaning that the dead of both the 55th Massachusetts and the 1st North Carolina were buried together. The Morning Reports of the 1st North Carolina indicated that on February 3, 1864, Private Primus Rin died in the 1st NCCI regimental hospital. This reference noted that each regiment had its own hospital. However, the next entry stated that on February 4, 1864, Private Rin was buried in the brigade cemetery.[44] Since they were obviously together as a brigade at this time and camped next to each other, the cemetery must have been used by both units. This was the only documentary evidence mentioning a cemetery for the two units during the winter camp.

Thus, through a combination of facts from archaeology, archival history, and physical anthropology, the cemetery was positively identified as that of the 55th Massachusetts and 1st North Carolina Colored Infantry. Interestingly, long after this analysis was completed the relic collector who first identified the site to the archaeologists admitted that he had recovered the stencil of Pvt. Harrison Peril, Co. K, 55th Massachusetts, just west of the cemetery site.

Of course the reality of the past is never as clean and neat as archaeologists or historians portray it. For example, the evidence tends to eliminate further consideration of the 33rd USCI and the small detachments of the 2nd and 3rd NCCI. The 33rd USCI was on duty at Folly Island from July to November 1864, and again briefly in December of 1864. Its members were only in winter camp on Folly Island for a brief time.[45] Normally the regiment would have buried its dead in its own regimental cemetery, and this was probably true on

Folly Island. But certainly the 33rd, or any of the units that served on the island in the winter of 1864-65, could have had one or two members buried in another regiment's cemetery by the strange circumstances of war. In fact, that is exactly what happened to two members of the 2nd USCI. The 55th's Regimental Surgeon reported to the Massachusetts Surgeon General in December of 1864 that:

> In addition to the number of deaths in our own regiment, two privates of Co. A, 2nd Reg. U.S. Col'd Infantry, died in our hospital. They were on detached service; and as the Post Hospital on Folly Island has been broken up, they had no other place to go."[46]

The probable presence of these two members of the 2nd USCI in among the graves recovered by the archaeologists not only demonstrates the complexity of such analysis it also demonstrates the universal ambiguity of Civil War records and the difficulty of pinpointing the location of any one regiment at any one time. Officially, the 2nd USCI was assigned to the Department of the Gulf and never on Folly Island. But the surgeon's letter is clear that Company A, of the 2nd USCI was placed on detached service on Folly Island from August 1863 to December 1863, at a time when the regiment did not even formally exist.[47]

After the recovery of the brigade cemetery, community interest focused on the surrounding site and further archaeological work was deemed necessary when the developer applied for construction permits to complete the residential development. The archaeologists returned once more to the archives and to Folly Island to excavate portions of the campground near the site. While the intense and overlapping use of the area by many units made it impossible to sort which archaeological features belonged to which individual unit, what we found presented a vivid picture of life and death on Folly Island during the Civil War.

Life and Death on Folly Island

When Wild's African Brigade landed on Folly Island, its members had no idea that for the next six months they would be subjected to a Spartan life of exhaustive labor, excessive heat, boredom, tension and fear. Today, Folly Island is a quiet six-mile long barrier island with the Atlantic on its eastern shores and a scenic marshlands hugging its western shoreline. This long thin dash of an island—it is only three-quarters of a mile wide at its widest point—consists of high undulating sand dunes, wide beaches and thick inland woods of palmetto, scrub oak and pine. It was even more beautiful and quiet in 1863 with only one major landmark, a plantation house, on the southern end. The arrival of thousands of Union soldiers that August transformed the island into a cramped, noisy and wretched place. One soldier wrote home "A man in civil life must indeed be a fool to think he could live on such a baron [sic] place."[48]

This soldier was not alone in his assessment of island life. The Northerners had been dropped onto a hot humid isle of sand to dig fortifications and haul cannon, with no time to acclimate. "Folly Island was probably the worst place in the army," complained a New York trooper. "If there is a worse place than these islands I don't want to see it."[49] The only relief from the summer heat was the evening breezes on the beach, and troops camped there for that reason. During the day, however, life on the beach in heavy blue uniforms was very unpleasant. "Our exposure to the excessive heat of the day," explained another soldier, "rapidly reduced the physical tone of the organization."[50]

Sand and insects plagued the soldiers. "If you fell asleep, on waking your face would be covered, your clothes were full [of sand]" wrote William Hyde.[51] "The greatest annoyance experienced was from the immense clouds of fine sand which penetrated everywhere, and covered whatever eatables we had."[52] Mosquitos were especially nerve-wracking, and "even overcoats [were] no protection from the ravenous. . . hoard of blood suckers. . .stinging, buzzing. . .screaming. . .dashing into your ears, wearing a fellows life out with coughing, slapping, pinching, and scratching."[53] Sand fleas and ticks added to the soldier's misery. There were also the ever-present flies. Assistant Surgeon Burt Wilder of the 55th Massachusetts noted that "The flies here are very greedy and undiscriminating; they will remain on a morsel till it actually enters the mouth, and they plunge headlong into ink and other unsuitable liquids; they can bite severely too."[54] Wilder, an avid naturalist, discovered more dangers of the beach:

> Yesterday a man suddenly dropped something that he was carrying and Lt. Thurber took it on a stick to the Q.M.'s tent. . . .It was a 'Portuguese Man-of-War,'. . .I put it in a basin of water without touching the tentacles. After examining it about ten minutes I felt a stinging over the back of that hand, especially the middle joints of the fingers. This steadily increast, extending up the arm, and finally reacht my chest so that on that side I could scarcely breath; this lasted for about an hour; and the pain in the arm gradually ceased.[55]

On the other hand, camping on the beaches wasn't total privation. "Men and officers bathe a good deal," wrote one soldier, "but the beach slopes so gradually that the surf is pretty far out and there is some fear of sharks."[56] In

Assistant Surgeon Burt Wilder
55th Massachusetts

Department of Manuscripts and University Archives, Cornell University Library, Ithaca, NY

fact, Surgeon Wilder, his duties to the sick excusing him from the hard labor that his men and other officers endured, had an entirely different perspective on the regiments' beach-side residence:

> Just before supper the Q.M., Major, Captains Crane and Goodwin and myself had a magnificent surf bath; the waves were very high, higher than our heads, and I was overwhelmed several times. This is the finest beach I every saw, and were other conditions in keeping with our stay here might be regarded as a delightful summer outing.[57]

The soldier's fear of sharks was real. "Our camp is in the midst of the sand hills on the beach of the Atlantic, whose roaring breakers I hear tumbling on the shore, as I sit here writing," wrote a Union Sergeant. "The boys have already caught a crocodile weighing eleven hundred pounds and one of them has been so unlucky as to have his leg bit off by a shark. The position is a healthy one."[58] Despite the dangers the soldiers looked forward to their chance to swim, except perhaps in one instance. The men of the 55th Massachusetts took an unexpected dip when their commander Colonel Hartwell decided to teach a desk-jockey from headquarters a lesson:

> Littlefield knew nothing of tactics and depended upon his adjutant (Robinson by name) to post him as to the proper command and orders to give. One day on the smooth beach of Folly Island he decided to have brigade drill, and taking his points from Robinson, who knew but little more than his Chief, the order was given that turned the 55th Regiment right into the sea. Colonel Hartwell never stopped and the men were waist deep when Littlefield shouted "Hartwell stop, stop!!, but Hartwell only replied 'give the proper order,' but poor Littlefield did not know what order to give and his Adjutant was just as befogged.[59]

Hartwell eventually halted the men while Littlefield left the field, thoroughly taken down.

Hard as it was, drill was probably one of the least taxing duties the soldiers endured. According to the unit's regimental history:

> From Aug. 10 until the opening fire upon Fort Sumter, Sept. 5, 1863, heavy details for both night and day fatigue were made from the regiment, amounting on the average to at least three hundred and fifty men each twenty-four hours. These details were employed in cutting timber, making gabions, building wharves, loading and unloading stores, artillery, and ammunition, hauling heavy guns to the front, and working in the trenches on Morris Island. The greater part of the work was under fire.[60]

Whites and blacks both worked hard during that summer and fall. A New York soldier wrote home that these work details sometimes lasted 36 to 48 hours straight with little or no rest. Once, they labored for 60 hours without rations. General Vogdes was working the black troops especially hard, to the point that Surgeon Wilder complained:

> Brig. Gen Vogdes, in command of the island, called while I was studying our sick list this morning and said it was too large; and hoped I did not allow men to impose upon me and when not really ill; it makes me somewhat indignant for he has been taking our men, 400 or 500 at a time, and many of them have been out four or five nights in succession at hardwork; I am determined that none shall go who are unfit.[61]

The tasks imposed upon the soldiers were often dangerous. Cutting trees, hauling cannon and digging fortifications exposed the men to painful and potentially crippling accidents. Surgeon Wilder's diary often referred to the treatment of accident victims:

> . . .there are several minor surgical cases under my care just now; a toe nearly crushed off, a finger crushed yesterday, a foot that had to be lanced this morning, and a hand accidentally shot a few days ago; the man whose arm was dislocated some time ago has been on duty for several days.[62]

Totally exhausted by labor and training, the men were also forced to endure the tedium and anxiety of guard duty. Their anxiety grew as much from the presence of the enemy as their own officers. No one on the picket line could sleep, lay or sit down. The penalty for sitting down was to be hung by the thumbs. Falling asleep on guard duty meant execution. When the cannonade against Fort Sumter began in the fall, the day began especially early:

> . . .in addition to guard, picket, and fatigue duty, the whole regiment was required to be under arms at four a.m., and to remain until daybreak. . . .It was considered very unhealthy for the men to stand still or lie down in the open air before sunrise, and the regiment was frequently drilled upon the beach, by company or battalion, during this morning hour.[63]

Notwithstanding the vacation atmosphere that Surgeon Wilder was experiencing, morale among the soldiers on Folly Island continued to decline during the summer. "We looked every hour upon the same naked beaches of sand, the same drooping palmettos," wrote one despondent soldier.[64] Most were away from home for the first time and homesickness, or "nostalgia" as the physicians termed it, was acute. "[An] indescribable shadow. . .overhung and pervaded our organization," one soldier remembered. "The men [were in] a negative mood, never seen in the regiment before. . ." wrote another in the 117th New York.[65]

Naturally, the soldier's main target for complaints was their commander. "It is the general opinion that [Vogdes] is the meanest man alive," stated one trooper. "He is the greatest coward in the Army; keeps a whole company to guard his headquarters, and dares not go out after dark."[66] Officers were not the only targets for enlisted abuse. Bored troopers on the northern end of Folly Island also took a let fly a few pot-shots at their own men on Morris Island across the inlet.

Fortunately morale changed to a remarkable extent as the weather cooled through the fall. With the gun emplacements built and the siege continuing at a slower pace, duties were less arduous. The men, who had only a few months earlier complained bitterly about duty on Folly Island, became more content, finding the island "quite a healthy place"[67] One officer in the 117th New York wrote that "The men were cheerful. . .and vivacious."[68] For the 55th Massachusetts and the 1st North Carolina, conditions improved considerably with their move to the winter camp on the back of Folly Island. Sergeant White with the 55th referred to the winter camp as ". . .our then very pleasant camp."[69]

Perhaps one reason for the improvement in morale was the better quality water discovered inland away from the beach. Finding drinkable water was a constant problem on the barrier islands. With thousands of troops laboring in the hot sun, potable water was essential, and this need kept the soldiers forever digging wells. Most of the water was brackish and sulfuric. "The water here is worse than miserable—brackish and unhealthy," was how one soldier described it.[70] The best water was found within the inland sand ridges that were close to the soldiers' winter camp. Surgeon Wilder, who took note in August of the "poor water," remarked after the move that "the water is better at this camp."[71] Whether the soldiers digging the wells into the dune-sides knew it or not, it was the natural hydrology of these large dunes that provided the most refreshing water.[72] Below these dunes were columns of fresh water reaching depths several times the height of the dune. A regimental history of the 157th New York described the process of obtaining drinkable water:

> All the water used on the island [Folly] was obtained by digging below tide-mark and curbing with barrels. The finest and best protected well in camp was made by cutting into a sand dune and making a winding passage to the water, thus placing the water continually in the shade and protecting it from dust and dirt blowing around the camp.[73]

We excavated three of these walk-in wells and found the description quoted above remarkably accurate. Passages had been dug into the side of the dune, and once deep inside, hollowed out with just enough room for the well head. The sides of these wells were made of open-ended barrels, stacked upon each other below the ground surface. The soldiers probably dug the wells by gradually working the barrels deeper and deeper into the sand while excavating out the center muck. All of the wells we opened had been purposely back-filled after use. These wells probably did not produce water for very long, and were thus back-filled by the soldiers for sanitary reasons. While filling them, the soldiers used them as trash dumps. We found numerous glass bottles in these wells, some cut evenly across their middle and glazed at the cut to be used as drinking glasses.

While the water quality was consistently poor, the quality of the food varied on Folly Island. Most of the time the soldiers were fed a staple diet of spoiled canned meats, molded hardtack and coffee. "I live mainly on rice, peas, mush, and molasses, with the inevitable hard tack and coffee," remembered one Federal, adding, "I have a good appetite."[74] Like the recovered bottles, ration cans used by the soldiers were also found, some of which had been modified for re-use as cookers or cups. Campaigning soldiers often took advantage of their situation and relieved local civilians of their possessions. On Folly Island, however, there was little or nothing to loot, a fact reflected in the type of artifacts we discovered under Folly's sandy soil. A lack of ceramic pottery, for example, was a strong indication that the soldiers were using standard-issue tableware and eating mostly what was brought onto the island in barrels and cans. All the archaeological evidence points to a very meager, spartan lifestyle. Given their

spare existence on Folly, one can readily imagine the soldiers' delight when they
arrived in Florida. Having lived for seven months on Folly Island, Florida was a
veritable garden of Eden:

> The orange groves near the camp were loaded with ripe oranges, rare flowers
> were blooming luxuriantly, the moss drapery that hung from the live oaks
> made comfortable beds, and pigs and chickens which had not deserted the
> town with its other residents, and cows straying loosely outside the lines, were
> put in requisition for the use of the troops.[75]

Eatables—beyond their normal hardtack and coffee—were appreciated from
any and all sources on Folly Island. Occasionally, the troopers diets were supplemented by the quartermaster. In October the 55th Massachusetts was given "Soft
bread. . .and vegetables. . .to prevent scurvy," recorded the regiment's historian.[76]
Other unexpected "gifts" arrived for the men. "This month, a gift was received,
from the freedmen near Hilton Head, of a quantify of sweet potatoes."[77] Like all
wars, packages were sent from the home front. The Soldiers' Relief Society
provided donations, including among other things, condensed milk, corn starch,
dried apples, jelly, lemon syrup, mustard, crackers, bottled tomatoes and honey.[78]

No matter how barren the island, the Federals soon became expert foragers.
The sea and marsh provided much needed protein and recreation. Fishing and
crabbing became popular pastimes. The 55th Massachusetts' regimental history
notes, "almost the only luxury obtainable in August and September was fresh
fish, caught by the men from the beach."[79] A typical diary entry from those
soldiering on Folly Island read, "Frank caught some crabs today and they were
excellent eating."[80] Oystering was also popular, and we recovered a number of
shells from the archaeologically excavated winter camp sites. These shells show
markings of being shucked with a knife, and analysis of their ligaments indicate
that they were caught and eaten during the winter months, perhaps during the
time Wild's Brigade was camped on the interior of the island. Oystering proved a
hazardous pastime for some of the soldiers. Both Sergeant Johnson and Private
Logan, Company F, 55th Massachusetts, were captured by Confederates while on
an oyster hunt.[81]

In an effort to improve the soldier's diet, the army issued General Order
Number 40, which provided that:

> Fresh meat is to be issued as often as practicable, and commanding officers,
> while near the sea-coast, will encourage such of their men as are off duty or
> not otherwise employed to fish during the cool hours of the morning and

evening. . . .In a scarcity of fresh meat those troops in the most exposed and unhealthy situations are to be first served.[82]

Solid evidence was also found that, at least some of the time, troopers were able to obtain meat. Butchered cow and pig bones were recovered from several trash pits on Folly. The butchering marks on animal bones from one trash pit indicated that the meat served had been quartered and dressed and was probably served in soups or as stewing meats. In another trash pit, however, we found evidence of prime cuts of beef: that is, the bones of beef and pig, transported to the island and slaughtered nearby. The remains of turkeys and sheep were also found. Obviously, someone enjoyed a good meal on Folly Island.[83]

Soldiers also supplemented their diet at the regimental sutler's wagon. Sutlers, who were loved for their goods but despised for their high prices, usually were considered scalawags who deserved the poor treatment they often received. Still, sutlers provided a long list of luxuries and necessities that the army did not issue. Some of these items and foods included apples, raisins, crackers, boots, gloves, shirt buttons, toothbrushes, pipes, razors, tobacco, stamps, stationary, soap, canned meats, vegetables and sardines, peppers, pickles, socks and magazines.[84] One can imagine that the regiment's improvement in morale during winter camp was partly due to the fact that:

> About this time, the stores of the regimental sutler, D.W. Johnson, arrived, much to the gratification of officers and men; for the former had been dependent for stores upon the sutlers and commissaries on Morris Island, which the distance, and restrictions on passes, made difficult of access.[85]

Sutler's also provided the men and officers with another necessity of soldier life: alcohol. The poor quality of the drinking water available on the barrier islands probably contributed to their desire and it is little wonder that we excavated a large number of wine, whiskey and beer bottles from the camp sites. In fact, the surface of one site we examined—possibly the location of a sutler's camp—was literally covered with bottles. Although sutlers were officially prohibited from selling alcohol, the regulation was evidently widely ignored by both merchants and customers alike.[86] A journal entry of an officer of the 104th Pennsylvania, assigned to enforce regulations on incoming sutler shipments during the siege, provides a typical example of the soldier's attitude concerning the alcohol prohibition:

A non-commissioned officer. . .came with an order for 4 boxes of wine and
bought 11. The provost-martial seized his whole lot and I suppose they will be
confiscated.

I had 4 bottles of ale given to me one of which I kept myself and distributed
the rest among my men.

The Provost-martial General by order of Genl. Gillmore seized goods of a
Mr. Clark Sutler. . .and have arrested him—goods consisting of ale, wines, etc.

I sold my mocking bird Dick for $60 to Sutler of 62 Ohio Volunteers. Rec'd
four barrels of ale in payment. . .I have turned over to our Sutler one barrel ale.

Cargo of sloop *Golden Rod* confiscated and unloaded at wharf. I had to be
very sharp to keep detail of 56th Regt. Pena. Volunteers from all getting drunk.
They broke open a number of barrels of bottled ale and started the sider barrels
to leaking. . . .A great many boxes were stolen—of wine. . . .One of Capt.
Holmes men boasted that he stole three boxes. The Capt. discovered one box
and appropriated it to his own use.

Mr. Clark, sutler on *Golden Rod* was released last evening. . .the whole of
his ales, wines, and cider were confiscated.[87]

Soldiers on Folly Island devised all sorts of methods for obtaining alcohol.
For instance, visiting friends often brought the spirit with them as a gift:

> Mr. Scudder went to Hilton Head last evening but will return soon. He brought
> me a box of ale in small stone bottles; I have never cared for any thing of the
> kind but this enervating climate and rather trying life seems to suggest its use
> and very likely it will do me good.[88]

While officers had many opportunities to obtain spirits, it was more difficult
for the soldiers in the ranks. One source available to the enlisted men was boxes
from friends and aid societies in Boston. According to their donation lists, many
packages contained shrub, cherry bounce, cravat, sago, rum, cider, whiskey, cur-
rant wine, bitters and cordials, all of which contained alcohol and must have been
quite welcome.[89]

In addition to its obvious benefits upon imbibing, alcohol was also the only
readily available anesthetic beyond various derivations of the opium poppy. Thus
regimental hospitals maintained stocks of liquor, chiefly whiskey, for assorted
medicinal purposes. While these stocks were readily accessible to officers, enlisted men required a "prescription" in order to sample the liquid. At least one
trooper in the 55th Massachusetts, well aware of this requirement, formulated his
own method of acquiring a "prescription." The whiskey, which was kept in the
assistant surgeon's tent, seemed ripe for the taking. "The barrel of whiskey is kept

in my tent," noted the medical officer. "One of the soldiers contrived to slit the tent and steal some by boring a hole; but I tracked him and he will be punished."[90]

There was enough spirits around the 55th camp that sometimes the officers became intoxicated. Surgeon Wilder noted twice that "Last night, after a visit from officers of another regiment some of our own became grossly intoxicated and the major put four of them under arrest," and "Lt. Fowler, our new regimental quarter master, was grossly intoxicated today and fell off his horse while at Pawnee Landing and again near the quarters of Col. Littlefield."[91] These men eventually resigned to avoid court martial.

Controlled, general issues of whiskey were sometimes allowed for the enlisted men. The regimental historian of the 127th New York recalled that on Cole's Island, the regiment was supposed to have whiskey sufficient to:

> afford each soldier a gill or two each day, presumably for medicinal purposes and chiefly to go against the effect of the miasma from the marshes, but much of the whiskey. . .was in some way diverted, with the result that the soldier lost his anti-malarial medicine, with the exception of about one gill per month.[92]

Besides alcohol, men on Folly Island found other methods of relieving stress. They played card games, like whist, and participated in ball games, quoits and gymnastic exercises. Sometimes they made up games, as did officers of the 55th Massachusetts. "Between five and six Col. Hartwell, Col. Fox, Captains Nutt and Thurber and I amused ourselves with casting a huge hammer with a handle three feet long," wrote Surgeon Wilder. "Lt. Mowry (whom I admitted above) excelled us all in the throw with both hands, but I was the winner with the swinging throw and the throw over the head."[93] In addition, soldiers collected shells and walked the beaches like ordinary vacationers do today. They also carved bullets, which were eventually lost for archaeologists and collectors to relocate 120 years later.

The men of the 55th Massachusetts also spent their precious free time learning to read and write:

> Two large tents have been erected and floored adjoining each other, making a room some 45 by 25 feet, with suitable desks and benches for its furniture. Evening schools have been established. The valuable accessions to the reading matter of the regiment, recently received from Massachusetts, have given us quite a library. . . .I find there are not a few in the regiment, who, although

never having been slaves, are unable to write their names, and many are unable to read. A year's experience in the army has shown them the disadvantage of being dependent upon others to do their writing and reading of letters; and they are now applying themselves assiduously with spelling book, pen, ink, and paper."[94]

The brigade's officers, including Surgeon Wilder, served as teachers in these schools.

Though some of the men of the 55th Massachusetts and many from the ranks of the 1st North Carolina were uneducated, like all men they still pondered the great mysteries of life. A common form of entertainment in the 55th was to engage in open debates:

About an hour ago, hearing a loud voice in one of the company streets I went to listen. . . .They were holding and out-door debate; it seems to have been in progress for several nights; the question was, which are the more attractive, the works of nature or the works of art. What I heard was very extraordinary. Each speaker seemed to wish to say all that he knew upon any subject. . . .Finally the subject was dropped for this, Which is the ruling force, the hope of reward or the fear of punishment? One speaker claimed that the incentive to our armies was the hope of accomplishing some good; but a rascal named Pelett declared that he had no hope of anything, but enlisted for fear of being drafted. . . [95]

The hopes and thoughts of the men of Wild's African Brigade were much like those of soldiers everywhere in every war. There was, however, an extra, heavy burden, carried by the men of the 55th and 1st North Carolina each day: the onus of prejudice. Prejudice was manifest on Folly Island in actions, words and deeds. Throughout the war the United States Colored Troops received the worst equipment, supplies and small arms in the army because so many high ranking Union officers thought little of these soldiers.[96] No doubt the neglect of the 55th Massachusetts' equipment left behind at New Bern, North Carolina, was due in part to the attitudes of those in charge. In addition, black soldiers were often given the worst and most menial tasks. They also were employed by the white troops to do tasks that the whites should have done themselves. This infuriated Colonel Beecher of the 1st North Carolina, who wrote to Colonel Wild:

They have been slaves and are just learning to be men. It IS a draw-back that they are regarded as, and called 'd___d Niggers' by so-called 'gentlemen' in uniform of U.S. Officers, but when they are set to menial work doing for white regiments what those Regiments are entitled to do for themselves, it simply throws them back where they were before and reduces them to the position of slaves again.[97]

This practice became so widespread that General Gillmore eventually put a stop to it. "While there [Morris Island] I read two of Gen. Gillmore's General Orders," wrote Wilder. "One prohibits the employment of colored troops to perform menial or unmilitary service for white troops. In one case they had been employed to form a camp and pitch tents for whites."[98]

On occasion black soldiers took racial matters into their own hands. One soldier of the 55th Massachusetts wrote to a black Philadelphia paper:

> While we were waiting with patience for the long looked for morning to dawn, some of the men got to rambling about, as is common among all soldiers, when [a white Irish soldier]. . .took it upon himself the prerogative of calling one of our men a nigger: this not going down well with the soldier, he was for using the stock of his gun over Pat's head. . . .Col. Fox ordered Pat to come out and give a reason why he should call a soldier a nigger, but, not being able to satisfy the COl., he ordered him under arrest, and sent him, accompanied by at least two file of good brave colored soldiers, to report to the Provost Guard.[99]

But discrimination came in many forms beyond name calling, and the most irksome to the black soldiers was the pay inequity. When authorization came to raise segregated black regiments, the recruits were promised equal payment for services. In Massachusetts this was $13.00 dollars a month plus rations, clothing, a bounty of $50.00 for signing up, plus $100.00 upon mustering out. In June 1863, however, the War Department announced that black soldiers would be paid $10.00 a month, three dollars of which would go for clothing.[100] This insult set off a fury of protest by the officers and near mutiny in the black ranks. Governor Andrew of Massachusetts even offered to make up the difference for the 55th and 54th, but to the former regiment, principle was more important than money. Numerous letters were written by officers and men of the 55th and 54th Massachusetts in an attempt to gain equality in pay. After continually refusing the $10.00 a month, on July 16, 1864, 74 members of the 55th Massachusetts signed a letter to Abraham Lincoln stating their case:

> We Have Been in the Field now thirteen months & a Great many yet longer
> We Have Received no Pay & Have Been offered only seven Dollars Pr month
> Which the Paymaster Has said was all He Had ever Been authorized to Pay

Colored Troops this was not according to our enlistment Consequently We Refused the Money. . . .we came to fight For Liberty justice & Equality. These are gifts we Prise more Highly than Gold For these We left our Homes our Fameleys Friends & Relatives most Dear to take as it ware our Lives in our Hands To Do Battle for God & Liberty. . . .therefore we Deem these sufficient Reasons for Demanding our Pay from the Date of our inlistment & our imediate Discharge Having Been enlisted under False & Prentence as the Past History of the Company will Prove.[101]

It took great courage for an enlisted man to write directly to the President, overstepping the chain of command. Yet even the wives of the soldiers wrote Lincoln. Rachel Ann Wicker, wife of Pvt. William Wicker of the 55th, asked "i wish you if you pleas to Answer this Letter and tell me Why it is that you Still insist upon them takeing 7 dollars a month when you give the Poorest White Regiment that has went out 16 dollars"[102] Eventually and in stages the issue was resolved. In June 1864, Congress authorized equal pay for all soldiers from January 1, 1864, and back pay to those who had been free as of April 19, 1861. This legislation solved the issue for most of the 55th Massachusetts, although at first they did not believe it. They also resented having to swear an oath that they were free as of April 1861. But there was relief among the rank and file and the officers once back payments were made in October of 1864. Many soldiers used the money to honor old debts:

For many months the sutler had sold to the men on credit. . .and every officer had probably done the same. . .It is not known that in a single case any man present with the regiment failed to repay his debts, often entirely forgotten by the lender; and the sutler's accounts were settled promptly and in full. Nearly eleven hundred dollars were raised by the men, without aid or suggestion from the officers, to supply the band and drum corps with new instruments.[103]

Finally, in March of 1865, Congress authorized equal pay from the time of enlistment for all black troops.

If life for the black soldier on Folly Island was often lonely and strenuous, it was also occasionally terrifying. Though Wild's African Brigade did not see combat during the summer and winter of 1863, its members were in constant danger of being killed by fire—especially as they toiled on Morris Island. Death could come at any time. One soldier from the 54th Massachusetts wrote about the constant danger of artillery fire. "Last Wednesday two weeks, while everything was quiet, the enemy opened fire on our camp from Sullivan's Island, and the second shell killed two men in my company while eating their dinner."[104]

Death more often came slowly. The 55th Massachusetts would eventually lose some 54 men in combat and four to accidents. However, they lost a total of 112 to disease, 63 while stationed on Folly Island. Diseases accounted for a large majority of the Civil War dead, and their toll on blacks was devastating. Approximately one black soldier in five died of the various diseases that swept through their ranks.[105] One of the worst of these maladies was typhoid fever, which took the life of 34 members of the 55th Massachusetts. Besides typhoid, the men suffered and died from chronic diarrhea, pneumonia and consumption. The heavy labor, heat and poor diet contributed greatly to the numbers who died. The army's move into the winter camp at the back of the island improved conditions somewhat and the rate of death from disease decreased. The 55th Massachusetts continued to lose men, however, and during the month of December 1863, 355 soldiers were treated at the regimental hospital. Eight of those men suffered from typhoid fever, 26 from Bronchitis, 13 from tonsillitis, 22 from diarrhea. Five of these never left the hospital.[106]

Far away from home and in a strange land, death on Folly Island was lonely and cruel. The realities of war hardened the men and made others accept its presence more readily, as Surgeon Wilder discovered:

> Last night I had an example of the readiness with which negroes resign the selves to death when ill. A man who has been long subject to epileptic fits and who never should have been accepted, had four the other day and has been ill ever since; he had four fits last evening and insisted that he should die and that nothing need be done for him; his comrades and even the nurse had the same feeling; but I insisted on doing what I could for him; he passed a very comfortable night and this morning thanked me heartily.[107]

There was very little that the nurses and surgeons could do for ill men except make them as comfortable as possible. As already noted, alcohol and opium-related drugs were given to relieve pain. More often than not it was the individual's personal reserves of strength and will to live, however, that determined the outcome, a fact that may have had a lot to do with why so many blacks died of diseases. Many came to war weakened by slavery and/or poverty, although they were not rejected as unfit as were white troops. Given the harshest duties they had few reserves to draw upon when they became ill.[108] Thus many died and were buried far from home.

Though 32 blacks from Wild's Brigade died during the winter of 1863, the deceased remained in the hearts of their comrades. A soldier of the 55th leaving Folly Island in February 1864 wrote down his thoughts as he sailed along Folly River on his way to Florida. As he did so, he passed the very spot where we would rediscover the friends he left behind:

> At daylight the order was given for all to come on board, and we were off. As we streamed down the river, I could see the many forts and batteries our men had helped to build since they had been on the island. There was one thing more I saw, as the boat glided down that beautiful stream, which caused me to take a hurried glance over the past. I think I hear someone asking, what was that? I will tell you. As I passed near the place of the regimental graveyard, I could not help thinking how many of our number we were leaving behind, whom we would never more see on this earth; those who had left their homes and home comforts at the same time I did, the young , the noble, and the brave, to fight for their country, and to avenge the country's wrongs.[109]

Reburial

On Memorial Day, May 29, 1989, the remains of the soldiers of Wild's African Brigade recovered from Folly Island were laid to rest once again at Beaufort National Cemetery in Beaufort, South Carolina, thus fulfilling a promise made to the city of Folly Beach and to the citizens of South Carolina. Both the archaeologists and physical anthropologists wished they had had further time to study the remains. However, after two years it appeared to be the right time to return the remains to the ground, where they could finally rest in peace.

Prior to the reburial the remains had been carefully prepared. The bones were wrapped in plastic and each individual was sealed in a plastic liner. Each soldier was placed in an individual black coffin, typical of the period, and the miscellaneous bones were collected in the last coffin to make nineteen burials. For the impressive ceremony each coffin was covered with an American flag with 34 stars. Reenactors representing Federal and Confederate soldiers carried the coffins to a specially-designated section of the national cemetery. At the grave site, speakers, including myself and the governor of Massachusetts, eulogized the soldiers and offered prayers. Taps was played and the ceremony concluded with a forty-gun salute. At last, the members of Wild's Brigade could rest, protected from further disturbance.

But what about the mystery of the missing skulls? Why did we find burials, carefully articulated in the ground, but with skulls and other bones missing?

Many possible disturbance agents were considered as explanations for the missing skeletal elements, including voodoo and relic collecting. Careful research, however, revealed that the most likely explanation was that the graves were opened and skeletal remains were removed sometime after the war as part of the general effort by the U.S. Government to re-bury soldiers in National Cemeteries. There is overwhelming historic documentation of this practice at other locations in the South, and even on Folly Island itself. The reburial of soldiers had begun—at battlefields like Gettysburg—even before the war ended, and by 1883, a quarter of a million Union soldiers had been reinterred in 79 national cemeteries across the country. Soldiers were often detailed to locate and remove the remains, but the government also hired private contractors.[110] For instance, at Gettysburg a "Mr. F. W. Bresecker [was contracted] to remove bodies from the field for reburial at the rate of $1.59 each, with no more than 100 to be moved on one day."[111] At Fort Pillow in Tennessee, the cost of exhuming 258 Union battlefield casualties and reburying them at a fort cemetery was $7.00 per body, with the total cost plus head-posts and fencing at $2,145.65. These soldiers were later exhumed and moved yet again to the national cemetery in Memphis.[112]

It is obvious that the contractor who first removed and reburied the soldiers at the Folly Island cemetery was very careless, taking only partial remains, and in at least two cases, missing entire burials. One such grisly scene occurred at Gettysburg, where one witness recorded that: "Many of the undertakers who were removing bodies, also performed their work in the most careless manner, invariably leaving the graves open and often leaving particles of bones and hair lying scattered around. . ."[113]

The likely explanation for the disturbances to the Folly Island cemetery raises the question of where the remains from the first exhumation were taken. In all probability they were removed to the Beaufort National Cemetery at Beaufort, South Carolina. A soldier of the 3rd New Hampshire states that soldiers of his regiment that died on Folly Island were removed and re-interred at the Beaufort National Cemetery. A history of Folly Island states that Mr. J. P. Low of Beaufort was contracted in 1867 and 1868 to remove bodies from Folly Island at the rate of $5.50 each.[114] There were already many markers at the National cemetery noting the location of unknowns of the 55th Massachusetts buried there prior to the Folly Island archaeological excavation. Therefore, it is almost certain that Low or someone else initially exhumed the remains at the cemetery we excavated and removed them, or portions of them, to Beaufort.

And so we have come full circle. Almost one hundred and thirty years later, the bones of the members of Wild's African Brigade who died on Folly Island during the winter of 1863 and 1864 were finally been reunited in the same cemetery, if not the same grave. As for their legacy, no better epitaph has been written than that of P. C. Headley, a Massachusetts author, who wrote of the 55th, "They added to the military reputation of the Commonwealth, gave strength to the Union cause, and forever silenced the clamor against them in advance by the enemies of the colored race."[115]

Notes

1. Recruitment Poster, U.S. Army 55th Regt. Mass. Vol. Infantry, Association of Officers Records, Massachusetts Historical Society, Boston.

2. Edward Longacre, "'It Will Be Many Days Before Charleston Falls': Letters of a Union Sergeant on Folly Island, August 1863-August, 1864," *South Carolina Historical Magazine* 85(2) (April, 1984), p. 124.

3. Stephen R. Wise, *Lifeline of the Confederacy* (University of South Carolina Press, Columbia, 1988), p. 122.

4. Patrick Brennan, *Secessionville: Assault on Charleston* (Savas Publishing Co., 1996), is an outstanding battle study and the first full-length work on this important early battle. For an excellent article-length treatment, see J. Tracy Power, "'An Affair of Outposts': The Battle of Secessionville, June 16, 1862, *Civil War History*, vol. XXXVIII, no. 2 (1992).

5. Benjamin Sheppard to his mother, June 22, 1862, Sheppard Family Papers, South Caroliniana Library, University of South Carolina, Columbia, quoted from Power, *Affair*, p. 168.

6. Chris E. Fonvielle and James B. Legg, "Chapter II: Historic Background,"in James B. Legg and Steven D. Smith, *"The Best Ever Occupied. . . ." Archaeological Excavations of a Civil War Encampment on Folly Island* (South Carolina Institute of Archaeology and Anthropology, Research Manuscript Series 209, Columbia, SC, 1989).

7. U.S. War Department, *The War of the Rebellion: The Official Records of the Union and Confederate Navies*, 30 vols. (Washington, D.C., 1890- 1901), series I, vol. 14, p. 437.

8. Charles Caldwell, *The Old Sixth Regiment, Its War Record, 1861-5* (Tuttle, Morehouse, & Taylor, New Haven, Connecticut, 1875), p. 61.

9. Ibid., p. 65. For a detailed history of the construction of the batteries on the north end of Folly Island and the later building of Fort Green, see Martha A. Zierden, Steven D.

Smith and Ronald W. Anthony, *"Our Duty was Most Arduous": History and Archaeology of the Civil War on Little Folly Island, South Carolina* (The Charleston Museum, Leaflet No. 32, 1995).

10. See Stephen R. Wise, *Gate of Hell: Campaign for Charleston Harbor, 1863*, (University of South Carolina Press, Columbia, 1994), for an outstanding and thorough history of the campaign against Battery Wagner.

11. Geoffrey Ward, Ric Burns, and Ken Burns, *The Civil War An Illustrated History* (Alfred A. Knopf, Inc., New York, 1990), p. 248.

12. Joseph T. Glatthaar, *Forged in Battle The Civil War Alliance of Black Soldiers and White Officers* (The Free Press, A division of Macmillan, Inc., New York, 1990), p. 3; Joe H. Mays, *Black Americans and Their Contributions Toward Union Victory in the American Civil War, 1861-1865* (University Press of America, New York, 1984), p. 1.

13. John W. Blassingame, *The Frederick Douglass Papers,* Series One, Volume 3 (Yale University Press, New Haven, Massachusetts, 1985), p. 596.

14. Charles Fox, *Record of the Service of the 55th Regiment of Massachusetts Volunteer Infantry* (John Wilson and Son, Cambridge, Massachusetts, 1868), pp. 1-2.

15. Fox, *Record*, pp. 110-112; "Interview with Hatch," March 31, 1895, Manuscript, U.S. Army 55th Regt. Mass. Vol. Infantry, Association of Officers Records, Massachusetts Historical Society, Boston.

16. Fox, *Record* pp. 110-112.

17. Ibid., p. 6.

18. Ibid., p. 2.

19. Joseph E. Williams, Published Letter (*Christian Recorder*, Philadelphia, July 18, 1863), quoted from Edwin S. Redkey, Editor, *A Grand Army of Black Men* (Cambridge University Press, Cambridge, 1992), p. 92.

20. Joseph E. Williams, Published Letter (*Christian Recorder*, Philadelphia, July 4, 1863), in Redkey, *Grand Army,* p. 91.

21. Fox, *Record,* p. 11.

22. Ibid., pp. 13-14.

23. 1st Lt. Clarke Remick to 1st Lt. William L. Manning, Adj. Report, January 1, 1864, 1st North Carolina Colored Infantry (35th USCT), *Records of the United States Army Continental Commands 1821-1920,* United States Army, Records Group 94, National Archives, Washington, D.C.

24. Dudley Taylor Cornish, *The Sable Arm Negro Troops in the Union Army, 1861-1865* (Longmans, Green and Co., New York, 1956), p. 268.

25. William A. Gladstone, *United States Colored Troops 1863-1867* (Thomas Publications, Gettysburg, Pennsylvania, 1990), pp. 113-118.

26. Fox, *Record,* p. 27.

27. Ibid., p. 30.

28. Sergeant, 55th Massachusetts, Published Letter (*The Liberator*, October 4, 1864), in Redkey, *Grand Army,* p. 68.

29. Fox, *Record*, p. 67.

30. Ibid., p. 42.

31. George Washington Williams, *A History of Negro Troops in the War of the Rebellion 1861-65* (Bergman Publishers, New York, 1968), p. 212.

32. Fox, *Record,* p. 44.

33. Ibid., p. 58.

34. Ibid., p 84.

35. Recruitment Poster, U.S. Army 55th Regt. Mass. Vol. Infantry, Association of Officers Records, Massachusetts Historical Society, Boston.

36. Legg and Smith, *Best Ever.*

37. Although they have since been revised, see South Carolina Code of Laws 27-43-10 through 40 and 16-17-600.

38. Ronald W. Anthony and Lesley M. Drucker, *Recovery of Burials and Construction Monitoring at Folly Island* (Carolina Archaeological Services, Inc., Columbia, South Carolina, 1988).

39. Charles Fox "Extracts from Letters Written to his Wife, July 23, 1863 to February 23rd, 1864" 2 Vols. (Massachusetts Historical Society, Boston, 1863-1865), November 17, 1863.

40. Ted A. Rathbun, Appendix A: Human Remains From 38CH956, In Legg and Smith, *Best Ever.*

41. Frederick H. Dyer, *A Compendium of the War of Rebellion* (Des Moines, Iowa 1959) pp. 1266-67, 1472, 1727, 1729.

42. Dyer, *Compendium,* p. 1729; *The War of the Rebellion: The Official Records of the Union and Confederate Armies in the War of the Rebellion,* 128 vols. (Washington, D.C.: Government Printing Office, 1890-1901), series 1, vol. 14, p. 437, hereinafter cited as *OR..* All references are to series I unless otherwise noted.

43. Fox, *Record*, p. 16.

44. Morning Reports of the 1st North Carolina Colored Infantry (35th USCT), *Records of the United States Army Continental Commands 1821-1920,* United States Army, Records Group 94, National Archives, Washington D.C.

45. Dyer, *Compendium*, p. 1729.

46. William Brown, Report of William Brown, 55th Massachusetts, Jan. 12, 1864, *Military Officer's Records.* Volume 6, Massachusetts National Guard Supply Depot, Natick, Massachusetts.

47. Thomas R. Bright, "Yankees in Arms: The Civil War As a Personal Experience," *Civil War History* 19, pp. 212-213; Dyer, *Compendium*, p. 1723.

48. Caldwell, *Sixth Connecticut*, p. 65.

49. Henry F. Jackson and Thomas F. O'Donnell (eds.) *Back Home in Oneida: Hermon Clarke and His Letters* (Syracuse University Press, Syracuse New York, 1965), p. 102.

50. J. A. Mowris, *A History of the One Hundred and Seventeenth Regiment, N.Y. Volunteers (Fourth Oneida)* (Case, Lockwood and Company, Hartford, Connecticut, 1866), pp. 80-81.

51. William L. Hyde, *History of the One Hundred and Twelfth Regiment NY Volunteers* (W. McKinstry & Co., Fredonia, N.Y., 1866), p. 50.

52. Fox, *Record*, p. 13.

53. Longacre, *Many Days*, p. 118.

54. Burt Green Wilder, Diary, Typed Manuscript, Wilder Collection (Division of Rare & Manuscripts Collections, Carl A. Krock Library, Cornell Unversity Library, Ithaca, New York, Sunday May 4, 1863 to Monday Sept. 4, 1865), p. 25.

55. Ibid., p. 20a.

56. Ibid., p. 13.

57. Ibid., p. 14.

58. Longacre, *Many Days*, p. 112.

59. Manscript Quoting Colonel Leonard B. Perry (Private Collection of Mary Hartwell Truesdell, Bath, Maine, December 1912) copy provided to the author by Kathy Dhalle, New Hartford, New York.

60. Fox, *Record*, p. 11.

61. Wilder, Manuscript, p. 16.

62. Ibid., pp. 29-30.

63. Fox, *Record*, p. 12.

64. Hyde, *112th New York*, p. 62.

65. Mowris, *117th New York*, p. 82-83.

66. Jackson and O'Donnell, *Back Home in Oneida*, p. 115.

67. Edward G. Longacre, Editor *From Antietam to Fort Fisher: The Civil War Letters of Edward King Wightman, 1862-1865* (Farleigh Dickinson University Press, Rutherford, New York, 1985), p. 158.

68. Mowris, *117th New York*, p. 87.

69. R. W. White [Sergeant] Published Letter (*Christian Recorder*, Philadelphia, April 2, 1864), quoted from Redkey, *Grand Army*, p. 37.

70. Longacre, *Many Days*, p. 116.

71. Wilder, Manuscript, pp. 14-43.

72. Douglas Green, personal communication, May 1989.

73. A. R. Barlow, *Company G: A Record of Services of One Company of the 157th N.Y. Volunteers In the War of the Rebellion* (A. W. Hall, Syracuse, New York, 1899), p. 158.

74. Wilder, Manuscript, p 15.

75. Fox, *Record*, p. 24.

76. Ibid., p. 15.

77. Ibid., p. 16.

78. Extracts From Ledger Recording Donations Received By The 55th Massachusetts Colored Infantry 1863-64, Manuscript (Colonel Alfred S. Hartwell Papers, George Fingold Library, State Library of Massachusetts, Boston). For an extensive listing of donations to the 55th Massachusetts, see Legg and Smith, *Best Ever,* Appendix D-5.

79. Fox, *Record*, p. 16.

80. Wilder, Manuscript, p 33

81. Fox, *Record*, p.18.

82. *OR* 14, pp. 457-459.

83. Lynn M. Snyder, "Vertebrate Faunal Materials From Sites 38CH964 & 38CH965 Folly Island, Charleston County, South Carolina, 1988 Excavation," In Legg and Smith *Best Ever*, Appendix B.

84. Francis Lord, *Civil War Sutlers and Their Wares* (Thomas Yoseloff, NY, 1969).

85. Fox, *Record*, p.16.

86. Daniel Eldredge, *The Third New Hampshire and All About It* (E. B. Stillings, Boston, 1983), p. 986.

87. Captain William Marple, Unpublished Manuscript (Private Collection of Dr. Stephen Wise, Beaufort, South Carolina), pp. 19-20.

88. Wilder, Manuscript, p 26.

89. Legg and Smith, *Best Ever* 1989, Appendix D5.

90. Wilder, Manuscript, p. 45.

91. Ibid., pp. 44-45.

92. Franklin McGrath, *The History of the 127th New York Volunteers 'Monitors' in the War for the Preservation of the Union* (Published by the Author, Thomas Cooper Library, University of South Carolina, Columbia), pp. 82-83.

93. Wilder, Manuscript, p. 59.

94. Sergeant, 55th Massachusetts, Published Letter (*The Liberator*, October 4, 1864) in Redkey, *Grand Army,* p. 69.

95. Wilder, Manuscript, p. 55.

96. Glatthaar, *Forged*, p. 185.

97. Ibid.

98. Wilder, Manuscript, p 29.

99. Sergeant 55th Massachusetts, Published Letter (*Christian Recorder*, April 2, 1864), quoted from Redkey, *Grand Army*, pp. 38-39.

100. For a concise history of the pay dispute, see Ira Berlin, Editor, *Freedom: A Documentary History of Emancipation 1861-1867, Series II: The Black Military Experience* (Cambridge University Press, Cambridge, 1982), pp. 362-368.

101. Ibid., pp. 401-402.

102. Ibid., p. 402.

103. Fox, *Record,* pp. 37-38.

104. Samuel A. Valentine, 54th Massachusetts, Published Letter (*Christian Recorder*, August 27, 1864), quoted from Redkey, *Grand Army*, p. 67.

105. Berlin, *Freedom,* p. 633.

106. Brown to Dale, Jan 12, 1864.

107. Wilder, Manuscript, p. 12.

108. Berlin, *Freedom*, pp. 634-637.

109. Sergeant 55th Massachusetts, Published Letter (*Christian Recorder*, April 2, 1864), quoted from Redkey, *Grand Army*, p. 39.

110. Francis A. Lord, *They Fought for the Union* (The Stackpole Company, Harrisburg, Pennsylvania, 1960), p. 328.

111. Earl J. Coates, "A Quartermaster's Battle of Gettysburg," *North South Trader*, 1977, vol. 5 (1), p. 20.

112. Robert C. Mainfort, Jr., *Archaeological Investigations at Fort Pillow State Historic Area: 1976-1978,* Research Series No. 4 (Division of Archaeology, Tenesseee Department of Conservation, Nashville, 1980), pp. 88-89.

113. Coates, Quartermaster's, p. 21.

114. Eldredge, *Third*, pp.1004-1005; James W. Hagy, *To Take Charleston: The Civil War on Folly Island* (Pictorial Histories Publishing Co. Inc., Charleston, WV, 1993), note 117, p. 82. Hagy cites letters from J. P. Low to Moses Sampson dated January 16, 1867, January 22, 1867, January 30, 1867, and letters to C. P. Low dated February 6, 1868, and April 23, 1868, in Letters Received Relating to Cemeteries (Department of the South, National Archives, 1867-69). The author has not seen these letters.

115. P. C. Headley, *Massachusetts in the Rebellion* (Walker, Fuller, & Co., Boston, 1866), p. 458.

Letter From Hilton Head, 3 June 1862: "With Gen. Hunter at the helm, the long-expected attack on Charleston is about to take place, and I have no doubt of the success of our brave fellows in the field. You can put it down as a dead certainty."[1]

PRELUDE TO SECESSIONVILLE:

First Blood on Sol Legare Island*

Patrick Brennan

In early June 1862, the long-delayed Federal attempt to take Charleston, South Carolina, began in earnest. Two Union divisions had garrisoned the Hilton Head environs since the previous November, but the Federal military minds initially had targeted Savannah, Georgia, and her river front, not Charleston and her harbor. After a snail-like three month campaign, the massive guardian of the Savannah River, Fort Pulaski, fell in mid-April to a day-long bombardment. Still, six weeks would pass before the newly arrived General David Hunter and his second in command, Brig. Gen. Henry Benham, acclimated themselves to their military surroundings and turned their eyes in Charleston's direction. Finally, on June 2, Federal columns descended upon James Island, Charleston's southern flank. Shocked by Pulaski's precipitous surrender and gutted by recent troop withdrawals, Charleston's Confederate defenders could do little but brace for the assault.

Although the Battle of Secessionville, fought on June 16, 1862, remains the key conflict of the resulting James Island Campaign, a number of smaller actions preceded Secessionville as the two sides jockeyed for position. One of the sharpest test of arms exploded on the second day of the invasion as elements of Brig.

* This article is adapted from Patrick Brennan's new battle study, *Secessionville: Assault on Charleston* (Savas Publishing Company, 1996).

Gen. Isaac Stevens' division attempted to secure their landing area. Three Federals regiments, the 79th New York, 28th Massachusetts and one-half of the 100th Pennsylvania, had landed on Battery Island on June 2 and pushed across to nearby Sol Legare Island, where they established their camps. Stevens, who desired an expansion of the bridgehead, ordered those troops already landed to reconnoiter further east at daylight on June 3. Meanwhile, his remaining regiments struggled ashore.

The Confederates reacted somewhat passively to the enemy thrust. Theater commander Maj. Gen. John Pemberton had ordered all of his forces back to an incomplete defensive line that ran across James Island, thereby ceding the landing areas to the Federals. Disaster struck during the night of the 2nd when Capt. C. E. Chichester's four-gun Confederate battery attempted to negotiate the rough footbridge connecting Sol Legare Island to James Island. Three of the four pieces plunged off the causeway and sank in the muck. Chichester's exhausted gunners failed to free the marsh-bound pieces, so Lt. Col. Ellison Capers and his 24th South Carolina were ordered to move from a camp near Secessionville to retrieve the guns at dawn on June 3.

With Stevens' skittish Federal force advancing from the west, and a determined Confederate regiment marching from the east, the stage was set for the Battle of Sol Legare Island.

*   *   *

Colonel Daniel Leasure arrived at Sol Legare Island on the morning of June 3, 1862, and accompanied the remaining four companies of his 100th Pennsylvania Infantry ("Roundheads") to their new campsites. The confusion of the landing zone made Leasure less than hopeful about unit-

Col. Daniel Leasure
100th Pennsylvania Infantry
Isaac Stevens' 2nd Brigade

Michael Krause Collection, U.S.
Army Military History Institute,
Carlisle Barracks

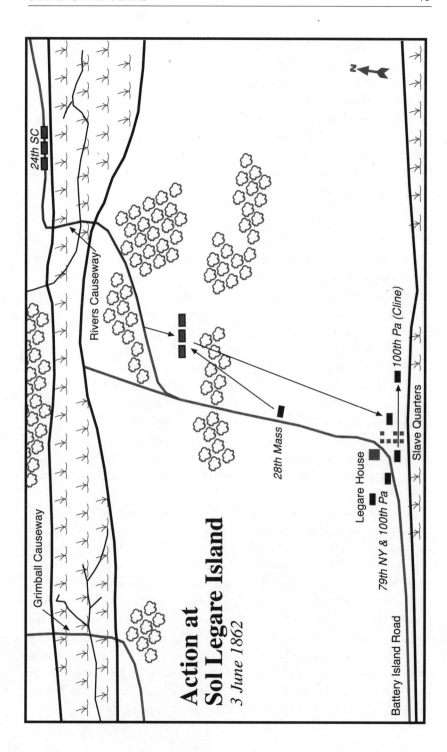

Action at
Sol Legare Island
3 June 1862

ing his immediate command with those Roundheads already camped somewhere out on the island. But soon after he arrived, while perusing his new surroundings, Leasure noticed some unexpected activity. Crews were transporting dead and wounded soldiers back to the landing area, and many of them were men of Leasure's own regiment. Arriving with these bleeding unfortunates was news of a sharp fight up ahead on the island, and the Roundheads were reportedly in the thick of it. The sight of these gravely wounded men, some of whom the colonel knew well, surprised the unsuspecting officer. He rounded his four companies up and moved them forward to their comrades' relief.[2]

*   *   *

Before he could continue the process of unloading his division, Gen. Isaac Stevens resolved to open the landing area by advancing those first troops ashore across Sol Legare Island. Therefore, at midnight on June 2, the 100th Pennsylvania received orders detailing 40 men from each company to report to Captain Elliot of the 79th New York at his picket post. Captain James Cline departed with the Roundhead detachment at 4:00 a.m., and soon discovered the Highlander pickets in the pre-dawn darkness. As the Pennsylvanians stacked arms to prepare breakfast, Cline found Elliot and received a briefing on the forthcoming operation, a proposed sweep of the length of Sol Legare Island. The Roundheads would join two companies each of the 28 Massachusetts and the 79th New York in spearheading the movement. As Cline shook his men out for action, Elliot aligned the Irish right on the Battery Island road, which ran along the southern border of the island, and pushed them forward into the underbrush as skirmishers.[3]

After advancing a short distance, the Northerners found themselves among the buildings of the Legare plantation, a clustering of structures at a bend where the road turns north towards the Rivers Causeway. The Legare house stood in the northwest quadrant of the bend. Immediately to the east, slave quarters rested between the marsh and a hedge line that ran parallel to and north of the swamp line. North and east of the Legare buildings lay a large cotton field bisected by the Battery Island Road. A stand of woods girded by a heavy hedge line marked the northern border of the field. The entire force paused briefly around the Legare buildings to survey the area, then Elliot advanced the Massachusetts detachment over the field toward the wood lot. As the Irishmen disappeared into the timber, the Roundheads forming a battle line near the Legare buildings ominously noted "unmistakable signs of the enemy."[4]

Popping rifle fire announced Confederate resistance to the movement. The Irish had made contact with the enemy somewhere north in the woods, so Cline advanced his troops to the plantation and formed a line of battle. The sounds of the fight echoed through the woods and across the field, warning the Pennsylvanians that hard work lay ahead. As the rifle fire drew near, the Roundheads tightened their grips on their rifles and peered into the distant trees for signs of their Massachusetts comrades. Within a half hour of disappearing into the woods, the Irish reappeared looking very much the worse for wear. Singly and in squads, the raw troops tumbled out of the woods while their officers scrambled frantically to retain some semblance of order. Just as the Irish succeeded in halting and forming along the hedge line, a blazing fire from the woods stung the nervous troops. "(T)hey broke and ran the first fire they received," wrote Cline. "This made things look like earnest." The Irish's precipitous retreat uncovered the Pennsylvanians, and as Rebels spilled into the field from the treelike, the 160 Roundheads realized that they held a defensive position of little advantage with a large enemy force forming for the attack. "In a few minutes the action became quite warm, and several were killed or wounded," were Cline's understated words for what followed.[5]

The Roundheads fell back to a rise in the ground just west of the Legare buildings and traded volleys with the advancing enemy while the Highlanders formed up on their left. Wounded soldiers lurched away from the firing line, and the dead lay where they fell. One small party of Roundheads pushed forward and established themselves around the Legare buildings. Most of the Irish rallied either behind the Pennsylvanians or among the slave quarters to the Roundheads' right, but Rebel skirmishers had taken advantage of the 28th Massachusetts' retreat by working their way towards the bushy marsh line east of the Legare buildings, opening a harassing fire on the exposed Federal right. Captain Hazard Stevens alerted Elliot to this danger, and Elliot ordered Cline to advance 20 men to cover the flank. Cline did so by establishing a position along the hedge line in front of and extending east from the slave quarters. This move took some of the pressure off the Federal line near the Legare buildings, for the Rebels now began to concentrate their fire on the smaller Roundhead detachment, making things warm for the isolated Pennsylvanians. With a small gap between his left and the Irish right, Cline was not happy with his predicament. He could easily see the danger of his exposed position and sprinted back to the main line to obtain reinforcements.[6]

The engagement remained static for some time as the two sets of Northerners traded shots with the Southerners bunched along the wood line. When

Cline returned to his squad with the reinforcements, the enemy suddenly sprang forward from their positions in two distinct wings and advanced across the intervening field. Led by a mounted officer, one column headed straight down the road at Cline's soldiers, while a larger group made for the Legare buildings and the gap in the Federal line. Despite the increasing pressure, Cline held his men in control, for he naturally assumed Elliot would fill the gap with the reserve from the 79th New York. As the charging Southerners closed the distance between themselves and the isolated Pennsylvanians, Cline discovered, much to his horror, that no Federal troops were moving to plug the dangerous rift in the line. Worse, both the Roundheads and the Irish around Legare's were falling back before the Confederate onslaught, leaving Cline and his small force, as he later described it, "to our fate."

Sergeant Robert Moffatt remembered Cline's shouted order for the men to "cut our way through" the encircling enemy. Cline's pocket began a fighting retreat, but the Rebels easily curled around their flank and bracketed the Northerners against the marsh. "They kept pouring volley after volley on us till within 10 paces of us," Moffatt recalled. "We were cut off and compelled to surrender," was Cline's memory of the event. As the small but hot engagement continued to rage, the Confederates hustled the 22 dejected soldiers of the 100th Pennsylvania—the first Union captives of the campaign—to the rear.[7]

*   *   *

Lieutenant Colonel Ellison Capers had led four companies of his own 24th South Carolina Infantry west from their camps in the pre-dawn darkness with

General Gist's orders to retrieve Capt. C. E. Chichester's lost and now marsh-bound artillery

Lt. Col. Ellison Capers
24th South Carolina Infantry

The Citadel Archives

pieces. When Capers learned from Col. Thomas Lamar at Secessionville that the Federal pickets covered the Rivers Causeway, he sought further instructions from Gist. The general ordered Capers to advance on Sol Legare "until the fire of his boats obliged me to withdraw," Capers later reported. The South Carolinian placed his men in line and marched west. Near the Rivers House, where the rugged Secessionville path met the Battery Island Road, Capers hailed the two companies of the Charleston Battalion that had drawn picket duty the night before. These outposts confirmed the increased Yankee activity just over the Rivers Causeway on Sol Legare Island, so Capers moved quickly. Ordering the pickets to fall in, he headed the entire force south and then west on the Battery Island Road, eventually drawing up before the Rivers Causeway. The Confederates found the upturned barrels of Chichester's cannon sticking out of the muck, but Capers knew he would have to clear the area of Federals before he could possibly remove the guns. Capers ordered his men into attack formation just north of the causeway and advanced Captain Sigwald and the Marion Rifles across the bridge to act as skirmishers. As Sigwald developed the enemy position, Capers rushed his remaining five companies by flank across the causeway and deployed them into line of battle, where they then "engaged the enemy warmly." The Southerners pushed the retreating Federals southward into a large stand of trees. In spite of the cover provided by the timber, the South Carolinians tore into the trees and blasted away at the increasingly disorganized Federals, who were desperately attempting to rally along the southern edge of the woods behind a hedge. For a short time they managed to hold on in this position, but the well-directed fire of Capers' men soon broke the line, sending them scurrying south across an open field towards the distant Legare plantation buildings.[8]

Capers reached the front and made some hurried observations. Near the Legare buildings, an enemy battleline "poured in a strong fire" on the assembling Confederates, "most of which passed entirely over us." Separated from this main line along a hedge line just east of the buildings stood a smaller force, whose apparent isolation made a tempting target. Capers determined "to cut off the advance from the support," by assaulting the gap in the enemy line. Aware that the Legare plantation was well within the range of the enemy gunboats patrolling the Stono River, Capers was initially unwilling to expose his men to such fire. But the isolated Federals dangled before him like forbidden fruit, and the young officer's fighting blood was up. As he put it, "I resolved to attempt it."[9]

Just at this moment, as both sides traded volleys, Capers received some welcome reinforcements. Learning that Capers was engaging a large enemy force, Lt. Col. Peter Gaillard led the remaining five companies of his Charleston

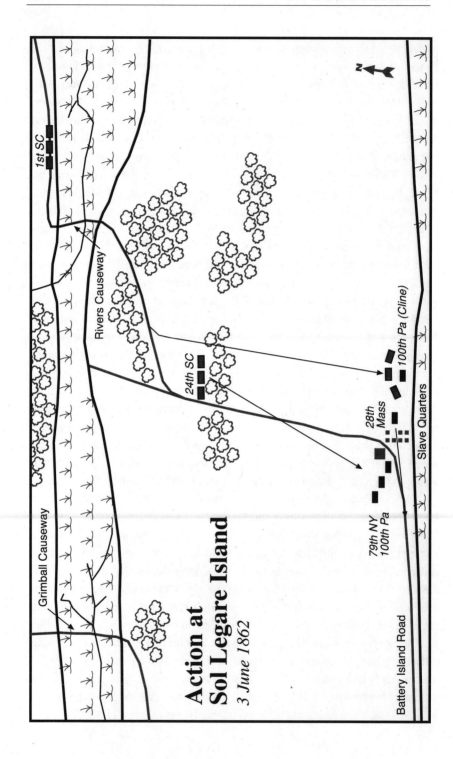

Action at
Sol Legare Island
3 June 1862

Grimball Causeway

Rivers Causeway

1st SC

24th SC

100th Pa (Cline)

Slave Quarters

28th Mass

79th NY
100th Pa

Battery Island Road

Battalion from their Secessionville camps to the "scene of action," mirroring Capers' earlier route. Gaillard and his men pulled up just as Capers had resolved to attack. Capers returned the "borrowed" picket companies to Gaillard and ordered him to move against the isolated Federals while Capers' own 24th South Carolina drove a wedge into the gap. Neither officer made many dispositions for the attack. Capers reined up before his regiment and called out, "I want volunteers to charge the enemy in those cabins. Boys, who will go with me?" The Confederates needed little goading. With Capers shouting "Forward! God and our rights! Charge!" the Southerners swept across the field. Capers' men sprinted hard for the gap between the two Union forces, while some attackers angled for the right flank of the main line.

The Charleston Battalion, attacking by flank in columns, bore down on the isolated enemy unit. Amazingly, the Union pocket stood its ground and offered signs of resistance, but the main enemy line retreated before the 24th's charge and fell back west the Legare buildings. One of Gaillard's officers, Capt. W. H. Ryan of the Irish Volunteers, led his company on the dead run against the isolated Federals, who were just then realizing their predicament and beginning to sidle westward. The momentum of the charge carried the Southerners into the gap, effectively blocking the Federal detachment's line of escape. The Unionists demonstrated considerable esprit and maintained cohesion in their dire straits, but the Charlestonians pressed forward and squeezed the Northerners against the swamp line. Captain Ryan, seizing the moment, raised his sword over his head and lunged at a blueclad officer demanding his surrender. As he did so, "a strapping Pennsylvanian" rushed the startled Ryan. Rody Whelan, a private from the Irish Volunteers, quickly jumped in front of the burly Yankee and twisted his bayonet "like wire." They locked in struggle until the "Irishman's trip of the foot" laid his opponent on the ground. With that, the Federal officer surrendered his remaining troops and resistance ceased.[10]

As the Charlestonians were mopping up the poorly-deployed Federals near the swamp, a mounted Capers led his own men against the retreating Roundheads near the Legare buildings. The Federals fell back to a point west of the plantation houses, but when the pursuing Southerners reached the buildings, Capers' earlier fear became reality. Shells from the enemy gunboats spun over the suddenly firm enemy line and landed with alarming accuracy near the Confederates. Capers recognized the futility of continuing the attack and, satisfied with the success on his left, decided to retire his force into the woods. With the Charleston Battalion providing support, Capers pulled the 24th South Carolina back from the buildings and reformed it under cover of the treelike. Having blunted the Federal advance while capturing a number of the enemy, Capers and his men felt confident that they had made the most of their morning's work.[11]

*   *   *

When the firing first started around Legare's that morning, the balance of the men from the 79th New York were busy establishing their base camp. Rattled horsemen reined up with news of the battle, and shouted orders called the New Yorkers to "fall in at once and hurry to the front." The Highlanders arrived about the same time that the Roundheads stabilized their line west of the Legare buildings. It was too late to save Cline's unfortunate detachment but there was time aplenty to take on the advanced Rebels. Two cheering New York companies rushed forward just as the Southerners around the structures "scattered. . .like chaff." The Highlanders pressed forward, but with so few troops in reserve, their pursuit was soon recalled. Much to the delight of the defenders, the Federal Navy had now had joined the fight. High over the 79th's heads, naval shells sailed through the overcast sky and landed with some precision amongst the enemy. The well-placed artillery chased the Confederates across the field and into the woods. With the disappearance of the Rebels, the firing along the line petered out.[12]

The accurate artillery fire was made possible by the superb communications between Signal Corps spotter Lieutenant Keenan and the *Unadilla's* gunners. Keenan had advanced with the Federal infantry and placed himself to observe both the Rebel lines and gunnery officer O. H. Howard aboard the ship. With their newly devised signal system, the officers could direct the shell fire with amazing accuracy. Even as the enemy disappeared into the wood lot, naval artillery continued its harassing bombardment, proving again the efficiency of the system that had been developed and tested earlier at Port Royal Ferry.[13]

*   *   *

As the Federal gunfire crashed down on the Confederates along the Legare field wood line, Ellison Capers knew he had overstayed his welcome. With enemy reinforcements advancing to bolster their battleline, Capers ordered a retreat to the James Island defense perimeter. Herding the Federal prisoners ahead, Capers drew his forces together and headed across the island enroute to the Secessionville earthworks. But, mocking their retreat near the Rivers Causeway in various states of muddy repose lay Chichester's guns, a mute reminder of the failure of the Southerners' primary mission. Evidently, no one considered that the Federals might make a dash for the valuable ordnance and succeed where the Southerners had failed, an oversight for which the Confederates would pay. Assuming someone else would effect their release, Capers left the guns where they lay.[14]

*   *   *

Soon after the Confederates quit the field near 11:00 a.m., the threatening skies unleashed a drenching downpour. From then until 3:00 p.m. that afternoon, the 79th New York and the 100th Pennsylvania watched the woods across the Legare field for any sign of enemy activity. Finally, just as distant Confederate guns began to fire from extreme range at the Union positions, two Highlander companies were ordered forward to reconnoiter the wood lot. The New Yorkers plunged into the dripping timber and followed the tortured curvings of the rough roadway. Not quite advancing a mile, they broke out of the woods and came upon a startling sight. Sitting in what appeared to be an open field were three upturned artillery pieces with nary a Confederate in sight. Flankers were deployed as the Federals warily moved forward. Along the marsh they found a wounded Highlander, "Clark of Company G," nearly dead from loss of blood. He had lain near Rivers Causeway since the night before when his reconnaissance party had come under Confederate fire. The New Yorkers tended to their friend as best they could.[15]

The Highlanders found the three cannon firmly ensconced in the marsh next to the causeway. Some pulling and tugging freed two of the pieces, and both were soon rumbling westward on two improvised caissons with the wounded Clark along for the bumpy and no doubt painful ride. Efforts to free the third weapon were complicated when a Confederate force appeared north across the marsh. An accompanying Confederate battery opened on the Scotsmen from 500 yards, forcing the Federals back to the cover of the treelike. Fortunately for the New Yorkers, the enemy artillerists were forced to divide their fire between the retreating train and the hunkering infantry. Support arrived once more in the form of naval gunfire, again aided by land-based spotting. The shells crashed near the Rebel position and discouraged any attempt to close the distance. As a consequence, no harm was done to either group and the Highlanders withdrew in good order. Just as the retreating Highlanders overcame the slower train, a section of the 1st Connecticut Light Artillery came galloping up to support the operation, much to the New Yorkers' delight. The Connecticut gunners had spent most of the morning unloading their pieces on Battery Island. When Lieutenant Porter's section was finally landed and readied, they took off for the front to see what good might be accomplished. With the Confederate guns still barking at the Highlanders, Porter brought his section to bear and exchanged fire with the distant enemy. "(A) few well-directed shots silenced the enemy," wrote a somewhat biased Scotsman.[16]

As the New Yorkers rolled toward camp with their prizes, the Connecticut artillerists took their turn trying to extricate the lone stuck gun. Joined by a small detachment of Roundheads, Porter guided his men to the piece while Confederate sharpshooters made life difficult for the Northerners. Three times the Unionists managed to hitch up the cannon to pull it out. Three times the harness broke. Finally, under fire in a what one described as a "shower of bullets," Porter ordered his disappointed men to abandon their efforts. The artillery section pulled back from the causeway and wound westward towards the landing zone, but in the confusion a detail of artillerists lost their way. They were wandering in the drenched woodland when a Rebel bullet nearly clipped a sergeant's nose. He announced "with considerable earnestness. . .`I guess we had better get somewhere pretty quick.'" Eventually they rejoined their comrades in the withdrawal. Porter's soaked, hungry men slowly made their way back to the camps, arriving just as dark cloaked the soaking terrain.[17]

*   *   *

When the fighting first began on Sol Legare Island, Col. Charles Simonton's Eutaw Battalion was ordered to march for Secessionville. Although the Confederates arrived there too late to join Capers in the battle, the men could easily hear the sounds of the fight. The Carolinians fidgeted as they waited for orders, but it wasn't until Capers and his men returned with a group of prisoners that the Eutaws finally got their turn to join the engagement. General Gist split the men between Simonton and Maj. John Pressley, and then ordered them forward. Simonton's group was deployed to cover the Rivers area. Pressley and his four companies marched north on the Battery Island Road about a quarter mile before filing west towards Grimball's Plantation. After passing through a wood lot, the men formed in a ditch facing the Stono River just a mile away. There they remained until noon, getting thoroughly drenched by a rainstorm until ordered to redress the line to face south towards Sol Legare Island.

As Pressley's men marked time in the muddy ditch, Simonton's soldiers lingered near the Rivers house before moving north to join Pressley's detachment in its new position, but this alignment was deemed unsatisfactory and the original position facing Grimball's was reassumed. Through the course of these movements, Yankee naval fire fell haphazardly along the front but did little damage. As late afternoon arrived, a report reached Simonton that the enemy were attempting to force Rivers Causeway. Amid a "perfectly furious shelling" from the gunboats in the Stono, the Eutaws moved directly south to a position in support of the Preston Light Battery, which had deployed in sight of the Federal activity near the bridge. With their musketry and artillery fire aided materially by Thomas Lamar's guns in front of Secessionville, the Southerners thought they had repulsed a Northern assault on the causeway. Unfortunately, the poor visibility caused the Confederates to misread Yankee intentions. In fact, the enemy were making off with two of Chichester's previously-stuck guns and were even then unsuccessfully attempting to remove the third. The Confederates never did realize what was happening, and their misjudgment allowed the enemy to abscond with the two freed cannon.[18]

After the causeway threat subsided, the Eutaws reacted to a report of another enemy advance from the Grimball area by returning for the third time to their original, ditch-lined position. In the gathering darkness a well-aligned battleline appeared in the field to their front, but before the frazzled Eutaws could fire off a volley, someone fortunately discovered the advance to be Maj. W. H. Duncan and Johnson Hagood's equally bewildered 1st South Carolina Infantry. The enemy landings had proved crisis enough to relieve Hagood's men from their provost duty, although Hagood himself remained in Charleston to tie up loose ends. As the two units commiserated on the close call they received orders from Gen. Hugh Mercer "to hold the front during the night" and act as shock troops against the enemy advance that was "confidently expected early the next morning."[19]

Fearing that the wet weather had rendered many of the men's firearms unserviceable, Mercer also ordered his front line troops to discharge their weapons. Mercer's concerns were borne our when only about one in ten rifles were able to be discharged. Even this modest fusillade revealed the location of the advanced Confederate line to the enemy gunboats, thus bringing on a resumption of the nagging naval artillery fire that had plagued them earlier in the day. The condition of the men's muskets also jolted the Confederate officers into requesting fresh troops to bolster the line against the expected morning attack. Major Pressley drew the unenviable task of locating Mercer to make the plea. "After a very fatiguing ride and much inquiry," the major found the general at Rev. Mellinchamp's house, just east of the northern terminus of the Secessionville Causeway. After laying out the condition of the 1st South Carolina and Eutaw

Battalion, Pressley was asked by Mercer if the soldiers had bayonets. The major replied in the affirmative. "Well Major," responded Mercer, "tell Col. Hagood to use the bayonet in the morning." Pressley rode until daylight to report Mercer's firm command to the exhausted infantrymen at the front.[20]

While Pressley endured this soaking night in the saddle, those Confederates in the front lines, "wet, weary, and hungry-slept on their arms. The night tempestuous."[21]

*   *   *

When they were relieved at dark from front line duty by the now suspect Irish of the 28th Massachusetts, the various companies of the 79th New York were finally reunited in their new camps. The rough accommodations made it a memorable evening for one Highlander. Andrew Fitch recalled his first night on Sol Legare Island for his father:

> I spent the most fearful night. . .On my arrival at our tent, which was used at that time as a hospital as well as quarters for ourselves, I found four wounded men stretched out on the floor occupying at least half the space. The remaining was crowded with boxes containing our baggage and medicine stores. . . . The men were severely wounded and required constant attention. During the night the storm increased in severity the wind blowing a gale and the rain coming down in torrents. Finally the wind increased to threatening to blow off and leave the poor wounded exposed to the drenching. In the midst of all this confusion one poor fello was breathing his last-attended hourle by a woman who is acting as nurse for the 100th Pennsylvania regiment. It required all the force we had at hand to secure our tent, but we finally succeeded.[22]

The Highlanders had taken but one prisoner during the day's efforts, a fellow Scotsman from the Charleston Battalion. Sergeant Alexander Campbell, one of the 79th's color bearers, asked the Confederate prisoner about his own brother James, who had served in the Charleston militia before the war. To Campbell's surprise, the prisoner knew James Campbell and informed the Scotsman that he had been in the fight just that day. Continuing the brotherly exchange with the Highlanders, the Southerner blithely remarked, "Had I known I was to be taken prisoner, I would have worn my kilts." But another Rebel prisoner spoke in harsher and less fraternal terms: "In the inland towns, in every mountain pass and rugged ravine, at every crossing of the road, and at every fording place, your people will be met, and harassed if not overcome, till you will be glad to close the war and leave us in possession of our rights." In the pouring rain on this drenched island, soldiers from both sides stood reminded of family and friends, of nation and nationality. The roaring fires fought off the rain as fried bacon and fresh coffee served to revive the tired soldiers.[23]

Such camp comforts were hardly available to Captain Cline and his captured Roundheads, now consigned to captivity in Charleston. Their captors had hustled the Pennsylvanians across the Legare field at double-quick time through Federal rifle fire and naval shells. At least one captured Roundhead fell before his comrades' bullets. Sergeant Moffatt observed an artillery explosion that killed several of the enemy, although the Northerners remained unharmed by the barrage. The Roundheads were led across the Rivers Causeway, past the Secessionville works and eventually arrived at Confederate headquarters, where their names were taken. A strong escort marched them across the island to Fort Johnson, where the Pennsylvanians got a dramatic look across the Charleston harbor at Fort Sumter. Enduring the taunts of some gathered Rebels, the men were piled onto a ferry and transported to Charleston. One more Roundhead would later die in captivity from typhoid, but now, for Cline and the rest of his Pennsylvanians, the Charleston campaign was over.[24]

*   *   *

Major General John Pemberton, the Confederate commander at Charleston, had just concluded one of the more trying days of his life. As the reports of enemy landings filtered across his desk, he immediately started to redistribute troops under his command. From Brig. Gen. Alexander Lawton in Savannah, Pemberton ordered up three regiments and the talents of Brig. Gen. William Duncan Smith. From Brig. Gen. Thomas Drayton at Hardeeville, Pemberton ordered one regiment to be transferred to Brig. Gen. Nathan Evans' right at Adams Run. As far as Evans himself, Pemberton ordered the enigmatic "Shanks" to advance immediately upon the enemy. The orders to Evans were symptomatic of Pemberton's confused state of mind. Pemberton wanted Evans to advance simultaneously on Seabrook Island and Legareville. "Shanks" had sufficient men to attack one or the other, but certainly not both. Ironically enough, on this same day, Robert E. Lee requested a brigade of Georgia troops be forwarded to Richmond under General Lawton, explaining to Pemberton that the enemy troops opposing him were being siphoned off to reinforce the enemy in Virginia. Pemberton had hoped reinforcements from other theaters might be available, but

Lee's request doused that. One can only surmise the tenor of Pemberton's reaction to such news. It couldn't have been good.[25]

The frustrated Pemberton also ordered some of the Citadel's guns into the lines west of Newtown Cut, although he later allowed General Gist some latitude as to their placement and disposition. This exchange pointed out a serious flaw in the Confederate chain of command. In his excitement to organize a solid response to the enemy incursions, John Pemberton continuously went over the district commander's head, General Mercer, and gave orders directly to States Rights Gist, the local commander. Mercer and Pemberton met on the morning of June 3 before Mercer left for the front, where he and Gist organized the defense from the Secessionville area. Such a sloppy command structure could only breed confusion, as illuminated by the Eutaw Battalion's gyrations and the loss of Chichester's guns. Pemberton did his best to juggle his resources and assure his soldiers at the front that reinforcements, including the Citadel Cadets under Maj. J. B. White, were on the way. However, June 3, 1862, despite the late morning capture of 22 Federals, had been a chaotic, exhausting day for the defenders of James Island.[26]

*   *   *

While Rebel and Yankee alike spent June 3 blasting away at each other over the Legare fields and the Rivers Causeway, harrowing adventures occupied the Northern soldiers attempting to disembark during the fierce, summer storm. The 8th Michigan spent Tuesday morning out near the bar, trying to transfer from the *Alabama* to a smaller vessel, the *General Burnside*. The high seas made the transfer impossible, so a flotilla of smaller boats buzzed back and forth between the two vessels, ferrying Michiganders now forced to face the prospect of drowning. When the transfer was finally completed, the *Burnside* fought rough water and driving rain to deliver the regiment to Battery Island. As the troops disembarked, ten men from each company were detailed to ride the *Burnside* back to Stono Inlet to obtain rations from the *Cosmopolitan*. Michigan Pvt. Benjamin Pease joined the group that drew this assignment. The *Burnside* steamed south but had to turn back when the heavy swells made docking with the larger ship impossible. Again, Pease and his compatriots weathered the ride to Battery Island only to be ordered again to ply the Stono to get rations. Near 4:00 p.m., as the *Burnside* approached her rendezvous, the captain of the *Cosmopolitan* shouted over the raging torrent to stay away. The *Burnside's* skipper turned to tell the hungry men that there was nothing he could do, but changed his mind when the 8th Michigan's quartermaster put a pistol to his head. The beleaguered captain chose expediency and ran his vessel alongside the *Cosmopolitan* while his opposite shouted "until he was black in the face: 'Keep away from me. Keep away from me.'" Suddenly, a wave lifted the smaller craft high in the air and crashed her into the massive *Cosmopolitan*, crushing the *Burnside's* starboard forequarter while slamming the captain and the quartermaster to the deck. The *Burnside* gave up the effort and left empty-handed.[27]

The steamer returned to dock at Battery Island and wait out the raging storm. Pease found some comfort by dozing on a coil of rope, but his detail was soon roused to march off to the 8th Michigan's new camp. The private searched for his comrades while wading through standing water up to two feet deep before he finally found his regiment with "no tents up and the rain just pouring down." At midnight, Col. William Fenton rode up to his miserable charges and asked for volunteers to bolster the picket line. Evidently suffering little from his exploits, Pease shouldered his rifle and joined the detail struggling off into the gloom, a very long way from the comfort of the Beaufort environs, a lifetime from the farms and forests of Michigan.[28]

*   *   *

More blood would be shed as the James Island Campaign played out in the rainy Carolinian summer of 1862. Numerous small contests flared in the days following the first clash of arms on Sol Legare Island. Another battle erupted on June 10 when John Pemberton foolishly pushed a brigade against the Federal entrenchments ringing the Grimball Plantation. The movement ended in disaster. Finally, on the 16th of June, Federal Brig. Gen. Henry Benham launched the divisions of Isaac Stevens and Horatio Wright towards the Confederate defenses fronting the planter village of Secessionville. The Southern guns that ravaged the Federal formations sounded the death knell of the Federal campaign.

After their signal defeat on the ramparts of the Tower Battery, the Northerners departed James Island in early July, little knowing that in the long course of the war, the James Island Campaign would be the closest they would come to taking Charleston. And although the carnage of Secessionville would be seared in the minds of the men who fought there, they did not forget the first blood on Sol Legare.

Notes

1. "Jordan," June 3, 1862 "Letter from Hilton Head," *Boston Herald*, June 17, 1862.

2. Daniel Leasure to "My dear wife," Daniel Leasure Papers, M. Gyla McDowell Collection, Pennsylvania State University, June 4, 1862 for Colonel Leasure's arrival.

3. William Gavin, *The 100th Regiment Pennsylvania Volunteers* (Dayton, 1989), pp. 84-85 for details of the early morning advance.

4. The best map of 1862 Sol Legare Island accompanied Col. Edward Serrell's official report to the chief engineer of the army dated July 7, 1862. This map, which identifies the area north and east of the Legare buildings as a cotton field, can be found in file 1.107 Civil War Maps/National Archives. The location of the Legare house (which is not on the Serrell map) is best given in Ripley, Warren, ed., *Siege Train, The Journal of a Confederate Artilleryman in the Defence of Charleston* (Columbia, S.C., 1986), pp. 143, 145, and 194. Gavin, *100th Pennsylvania*, p. 86 for Cline's version of the same and "unmistakable. . ."

5. Ibid., for "(T)hey broke. . ." and "In a few. . ."

6. Ibid., pp. 85-87 for further details. Hazard Stevens describes this action, including the makeup of the Federal line, in *Papers of the Military Historical Society of Massachusetts*, vol.9, pp. 135-136, hereafter referred to as "Stevens, PMHSM." Roundhead Thomas Williams, in Thomas Williams Collection, USAMHI, p. 25, recalled that the 28th Massachusetts "fell back in confusion rallying behind us" before the Pennsylvanians fell back "behind a small rise." After engaging the Confederates for a time, Williams joined "A small party. . .ordered to advance to the houses."

7. Gavin, *100th Pennsylvania*, pp. 85-87 for continued details; p. 85 for "cut. . ." and "They kept. . ."; p. 87 for "to. . ." and "We were. . ." Stevens, *The Life of Isaac Ingalls Stevens* (Boston, 1900), p. 391, for the Rebel skirmishers on the marshline and the presence of a mounted officer leading the attack. Stevens, PMHSM, p. 135, for Stevens' view of the Roundhead movements. On p. 136, Stevens describes the Confederate attack ("they charged down the road.") as taking a generally north to south direction. No map of the actual battle has surfaced.

8. U. S. War Department, *The War of the Rebellion: The Official Records of the Union and Confederate Armies*, 128 vols. (Washington, D.C.: Government Printing Office, 1882-1900), Series I, Vol. 14, p. 29, for Capers' report of his advance, "until. . ." and "engaged. . ." See Walter Capers, *The Soldier-Bishop Ellison Capers* (New York, 1912), p. 53 for Lamar's warning.

9. *OR* 14, p. 29 for "poured. . . ," "most. . . ," "to cut. . . ," and "I resolved. . ." In his report, Capers describes the isolated Federals as lining "the long hedge to the east" of the Legare buildings.

10. Ibid., p. 31 for "scene. . ." and pp. 30-31 for Gaillard's report. Capers, *The Soldier-Bishop*, pp. 53-54, for Caper's short exhortation and the beginning of the charge. NA, *Irish volunteers* (Charleston, 1878), p. 27 for "a strapping. . ."; "like wire"; and "an Irishman's. . ." Also see *Charleston Mercury*, June 4, 1862, for further details of the engagement.

11. *OR* 14, p. 30 for Capers' thinking; p. 31 for Gaillard's report, including Walker's wounding. *Charleston Mercury*, June 4, 1862, for Bresnan's wounding and Yankee artillery fire; Capers, *The Soldier Bishop*, p. 54.

12. Todd, *The 79th Highlanders, New York Volunteers in the War of the Rebellion* (Albany, 1886), pp. 139-140 for "fall in. . .," and for further details of the Highlanders movements. See *New York Herald*, June 24, 1862 for "scattered. . ." and the capturing of the wounded officer.

13. *OR* 14, pp. 27-28 for Howard's report.

14. Ibid., p. 30, for Capers' retreat.

15. Todd, *The 79th Highlanders*, p. 140 for "Clark. . ." and details of the afternoon advance. However, William Gage of Co. A, *New York Herald*, June 24, 1862, claimed that "In this charge we lost one man named Clark. . .who fell wounded and was taken prisoner, but was rescued by his own company." Neither account dovetails completely with the known movements of the 79th New York on this day. It seems more likely that Clark had been shot the night before rather than having been wounded and captured in Legare's field on June 3, 1862.

16. Todd, *The 79th Highlanders*, pp. 140-142, for details of this confrontation, and p. 141 for "(A) few. . ." *OR* 14, p. 28, for Keenan's spotting. Herbert W. Beecher, *History of the First Light Battery Connecticut Volunteers, 1861-1865* (New York, 1865), pp. 133-134, for the 1st Connecticut's arrival and advance to the front. Especially interesting is Porter's conversation with Hazard Stevens: ". . .if we meet the enemy we will action front and drive them before us."

17. Ibid., pp. 134-135, for this confrontation. Ibid., p. 135 for "shower. . ." and "with considerable. . ."

18. John G. Pressley, "The Wee Nee Volunteers of Williamsburg District, South Carolina, in the First (Hagood's) Regiment" *Southern Historical Society Papers*, vol. 16, p. 138, for "perfectly furious"; ibid., pp. 136-138 for Pressley's account of the Eutaw's confusing movements this day. Frank Moore, *Rebellion Record*, 12 vols. (New York, 1862-1869), vol. 5, p. 280, hereinafter cited as Tracey, "Rebel Diary," for Lamar's efforts and Gist's near-miss; Capers, *The Soldier Bishop*, p. 53 quotes Ellison Capers: ". . .why the regiments, which by that time came up and took position at River's, did not pull the guns out of the bog I cannot say."

19. Pressley, "Wee Nee Volunteers," p. 138, for the near-disaster with Hagood's men; "to hold. . ."; and "confidently. . ."

20. Ibid., pp. 138-139, for the weapons' discharge and Pressley's meeting with Mercer; ibid., p. 139 for "After. . ." and "Well. . ." Mercer was evidently unaware that Hagood remained in Charleston.

21. Tracey, "Rebel Diary," p. 280 for "wet. . ."

22. Andrew Fitch to "Dear Father," Andrew Fitch Letters; Lewis Leigh Collection, USAMHI, June 10, 1862.

23. See Todd, *The 79th Highlanders*, pp. 142-143, for Campbell's discovery and "Had. . ."

24. Gavin, *100th Pennsylvania*, pp. 85-87, for details of Cline and his men's capture.

25. *OR* 14, pp. 535-536, for Pemberton's orders.

26. Ibid., pp. 536-538, for Pemberton's orders; *Charleston Mercury*, June 4, 1862 for the reluctant Yankee prisoner (probably Captain Cline).

27. See Benjamin F. Pease, *Civil War Memoirs of* (Collection of Bill Compton, Oakland, California), pp. 31-33 for details of Pease's adventures.

28. Ibid., p. 33.

TO THE SHORES OF CAROLINA

Admiral John A. Dahlgren's Marine Battalions

Jeffrey T. Ryan

O f all the Navy officers under whom Marine battalions served during the Civil War, it was Rear-Admiral John A. Dahlgren's association with the Corps that proved the most long-lived. In his capacity as commander of the South Atlantic Blockading Squadron, the admiral's various schemes in 1863 and 1864 provided the marines with some of their most interesting and hair-raising employment during the course of the war.

In early 1863, Rear-Admiral Samuel F. Du Pont had command of the squadron, and with most of the rest of the South Atlantic coast shut down, was attempting to close off the port of Charleston, South Carolina. Charleston was considered by most Northerners as the cradle of rebellion, and Fort Sumter, in Charleston Harbor, had a tremendous symbolic significance for the Union. The Navy Department came to believe that the new ironclad gunboats were the tool needed to retake the fort. When Admiral Du Pont launched an attack on Sumter in April 1863, however, his carefully hoarded ironclad flotilla was mauled by the Confederates, who suffered little as a result of the attack. The primary result of the assault was to demonstrate that unsupported gunboats, even ironclad monitors, were not likely to bring about Fort Sumter's surrender. Nonetheless, the Navy Department was not happy with the result of Du Pont's effort, notwithstanding the admiral's earlier expressed doubts about the wisdom of the plan. On July 6,

1863, he was relieved of command of the South Atlantic Blockading Squadron and replaced by Rear-Admiral John A. Dahlgren.

Dahlgren's wartime service up to that point had been as Chief of the Bureau of Ordnance and as commandant of the Washington Navy Yard. He owed his admiral's rank to his ordnance work (he was a noted inventor and gunnery innovator), and to his close relationship with President Abraham Lincoln, who often turned to Dahlgren for naval advice. Navy Secretary Gideon Welles thought the admiral vain and ambitious, and Dahlgren's manner to his subordinates tended to distance him from their affection and loyalty. Even before his arrival there existed a certain amount of prejudice against him among the squadron's line officers, who resented the appointment of a "desk sailor" to so important a command .

Dahlgren was advised by Du Pont of the Department's instructions regarding cooperation with the army land forces that were engaged in attempting to reduce Charleston's seaward defenses, in particular Rebel batteries Wagner and Gregg on Morris Island, at the mouth of Charleston Harbor. Dahlgren rarely suffered from a shortage of ideas. On the 12th—barely a week after assuming command—he outlined to his adjutant, Cmdr. Foxhall A. Parker, a scheme for forming a "Naval Brigade" of three battalions, two of sailors and one of marines, to participate in special landing operations in the Charleston area. At first it seems that Dahlgren intended to draw the men he needed entirely from within his own squadron. In fact, the day after the assignment was given Commander Parker, all the marines that could be spared from the *Pawnee* at Stono Inlet and the *South Carolina* at North Edisto were sent to join the main body of the squadron at the entrance to Charleston Harbor.[1] It was soon apparent, however, that the admiral would have to look outside the South Atlantic Blockading Squadron for the men needed to fill out his Naval Brigade.

The Navy Department was supportive of Dahlgren's plan and tried to comply with his requests for more sailors as best it could. As for the marines, Colonel-Commandant John Harris was requested to put together a sizable battalion for Dahlgren's squadron to augment those marines the admiral planned to draw from his vessels off Charleston. On July 23, 1863, Colonel Harris informed Secretary Welles that he could assemble a battalion of 400 men from various stations, which he envisioned being divided into four companies, each with a captain and two lieutenants, along with an adjutant, an assistant quartermaster and commissary, and a commanding major.[2] The battalion was assembled in New York and the colonel hoped that it would be able to depart that city aboard the U.S. Coast Survey schooner *Arago* on the last day of July.[3]

Command of the battalion was given to Maj. Jacob Zeilin, who was to receive the marines designated by Harris at the Brooklyn Barracks. Zeilin was a native of Philadelphia with over thirty years in the service. He had been part of the relief column to San Bernardo Ranch and General S. W. Kearny in California during the Mexican War, and had served as fleet marine officer on Perry's expedition to Japan. More recently, he had been wounded with the Marine battalion that had served with the army at First Bull Run. His task was to organize the arriving marines rapidly into a battalion of his own before their departure for Dahlgren's squadron.[4]

While the commandant's estimate concerning the battalion's time of departure was accurate, his projection concerning its size was less so. Owing to sickness, desertion and the myriad other drains on the Marine Corps' limited manpower, only three companies could be mustered. The Marine battalion that arrived at Port Royal, South Carolina on August 5 numbered but 257 men under six officers.[5] Along the way the marines had been alarmed by a vessel that was at first taken to be the *CSS Alabama*, although it probably was an English gunboat. Major Zeilin's detachment was spared a repeat of the previous year's *Ariel* incident, when in December of 1862, a battalion of California-bound marines aboard the U.S. mail steamer had been captured by the infamous Rebel raider.[6] After obtaining provisions and transferring to the *Prometheus*, the battalion moved up the coast to Charleston, arriving the next day. The reduced numbers of the battalion sent by Colonel Harris did not seem to cause Admiral Dahlgren much anxiety, for the same day the marines arrived the admiral sent word to Secretary Welles that he intended to match their numbers with marines drawn from his squadron and thereby "organize a regiment."[7] Major Zeilin was assigned the task of deciding how many marines could safely be detached from each of the squadron's larger vessels, leaving only a minimum for shipboard police duties.[8]

Upon their arrival, the marines of Zeilin's battalion were quartered throughout the squadron on the larger vessels, but they were soon transferred to a camp of their own on the beach at Morris Island. There, the marines were among the navy and army troops conducting siege operations against the Rebel bastion of Battery Wagner. The Marine battalion was placed in support of a battery of Regulars from the 1st U. S. Artillery that came to be known as the "Marine Battery"; the navy had their own earthwork battery deployed, manned by sailors.[9] After a few days' inspection of the Marine ships' guards among Dahlgren's squadron, Zeilin made his report to the admiral. The major recommended detaching a force of 245 marines, drawn from 11 of the larger vessels, but mostly from the *Wabash*, *Vermont*, *New Ironsides* and *Powhatan*, for duty with his battalion.

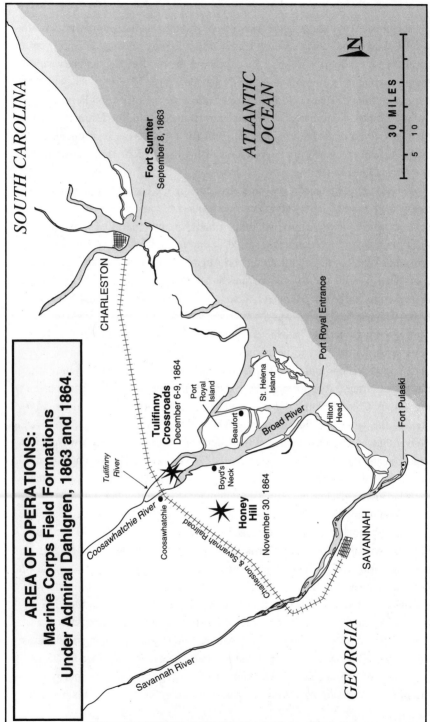

AREA OF OPERATIONS:
Marine Corps Field Formations
Under Admiral Dahlgren, 1863 and 1864.

Map by David A. Woodbury

Along with the 257 marines brought from Brooklyn, this gave the battalion a respectable strength of 502 men.[10]

Admiral Dahlgren's inventive nature has already been noted. He knew what he wanted in his Naval Brigade and made a number of recommendations regarding its functioning, including the use of buckshot in the marines' muskets for "close action," and the elimination of the marines' distinctive white cross-belts, which he believed offered "too good a mark."[11] At first the intended target for Dahlgren's Naval Brigade was to have been Fort Wagner, with the sailors and marines landing in the fort's rear—between it and Battery Gregg—while a simultaneous general frontal assault was made by the besieging army troops. Fortunately for the marines, they were spared the danger of executing this risky plan when on the night of September 6, after a lengthy and effective bombardment and with the imminent possibility of a land assault from the Federal besiegers, the Confederates quietly evacuated their defenses on Morris Island. Admiral Dahlgren, who now believed Fort Sumter at last indefensible, confidently demanded that the Rebels give it up. The Union overture regarding surrender of the fort was rebuffed, however, and Sumter became the new target for the Naval Brigade.[12]

Earlier, Major Zeilin had sent the admiral an extraordinarily frank letter regarding the future of his battalion. Zeilin argued that the marines under his command were not—or at least not yet—competent for the task expected of them, namely assault from the sea under fire. Most of the marines that the major had brought with him had been culled from navy yards, receiving ships and even a few sea-going vessels. Many of them had not been drilled one week before being assigned to his battalion, and the experienced noncommissioned officers needed to drill them were mostly at sea and unavailable. Marines were used to serving and drilling in small detachments, and so few of Zeilin's marines were proficient at company, let alone battalion, drill. They had no training at all relating to amphibious operations.

The marines' difficulty, the major noted, was further compounded by the weather. It was August 13 when Zeilin wrote to Dahlgren, only one month after the idea for a Naval Brigade had been first proposed. Temperatures were scorchingly hot along the South Carolina coastline at that time of year. Earlier that same day, an attempt at drilling the battalion ended when a number of marines were prostrated by the heat. Dahlgren himself was experiencing a marked increase in sickness among his sailors, particularly those unfortunates serving in the oven-like ironclads. Zeilin's main concern was with alerting the admiral to the fact that hopes regarding the efficiency of the marines in any landing operations in the near future might be misplaced. Dahlgren did not reply to the note, but whether as a direct result of it or not, the marines did not participate in any assaults for nearly a month.[13]

Unmentioned by Zeilin but nonetheless important was the fact that the sailors who were to have made up two-thirds of the brigade were even less experienced in their role than the marines. The men of the Marine battalion at least had the opportunity to live and work, if not drill, together, while the sailors were to be drawn from volunteers among the squadron shortly before an assault. The marines themselves experienced the baleful effects of launching instantly formed battalions into battle a number of times during the war. The inexperience of both components of the Naval Brigade in the type of operation that was expected of them was later to contribute to exactly the unfortunate consequences predicted by Major Zeilin.

Two days after the evacuation of the Confederate defenses on Morris Island, both Admiral Dahlgren and Maj. Gen. Quincy A. Gillmore, commanding the Department of the South and directing the army's efforts against Charleston, decided to attempt the capture of Fort Sumter by an assault from small boats. Their decisions were arrived at independently of each other and caused no small amount of confusion—particularly since the relationship between Dahlgren and Gillmore was marred by a frequent lack of cooperation. Two days before the Confederate evacuation, Gillmore's troops had made an aborted attempt at a landing near Battery Gregg in an effort to spike its guns and blow up the magazine.[14] The general now hoped to achieve success with an attempt on Fort Sumter. Perhaps since he had planned for such an assault since taking command, particularly with the formation of his Naval Brigade, Admiral Dahlgren rather petulantly refused to operate jointly with Gillmore unless the entire operation was placed under the command of a naval officer. As a result, the two operations remained separate but parallel.

Only a detachment of the Marine battalion, now under the temporary command of Capt. E. McDonald Reynolds, participated in the nighttime assault. Six officers and 100 marines, including fourteen noncommissioned officers, were selected on a volunteer basis for the dangerous task. Despite Major Zeilin's dire predictions concerning their readiness, the marines were eager for action, especially against such a symbolically significant target as Fort Sumter, and there was no shortage of volunteers among any of the ranks represented. The assault detachment was commanded by Capt. Charles G. McCawley, a competent and experienced officer in the middle of a distinguished career.[15] The marines were loaded onto their own launches and towed by the tug *Daffodil* to join just over

300 sailors and navy officers. As far as possible, the marine officers were distributed evenly throughout the various marine battalion boats. In the assault the
marines were to follow behind the boats of the sailors so that they might provide
covering fire for the landing. It was expected that somehow the detachment
would be able to simply walk or climb into the fort once they reached it. From a
distance Fort Sumter appeared to have been reduced to rubble. To Dahlgren, at
least, it seemed as though finding a way through the walls would not be too
difficult. Moreover, the admiral optimistically estimated the defenders' strength
within the fort to be "nothing but a corporal's guard. . . ."[16]

After a wait of several hours, the *Daffodil* and her charges got under way
with only the churning of the steam tug breaking the night's silence as the string
of boats headed for the dim outline of Fort Sumter. After approaching as close as
she dared, the *Daffodil* cast off the assaulting boats and headed back to the
squadron. The time was about midnight. From this point on, the plan, which was
not very clear to begin with, began to unravel. The Union force was broken down
into three divisions, one of which was intended to make a diversionary action
against the northwest face of the fort. When this had been achieved, the remaining two divisions were to launch the main assault on the southwest face. The
night was very dark, however, and soon many of the boats lost contact with each
other. A number of them followed the division making the diversionary action
toward the fort, thinking that this was the general assault. The order "pull for
Sumter" was given, but some of the boats did not hear it and instead milled about
aimlessly. One boatload of marines containing the battalion adjutant somehow
managed to maneuver itself back amongst the Union fleet, although it was
quickly sent on its way again with the addition of a compass supplied by the
admiral himself. Other boats, believing that the assault had been called off,
returned to the fleet. By 1:00 a.m., however, many of them had at last made it to
the vicinity of Fort Sumter.[17]

The Confederates had been prepared for the sort of attempt that Dahlgren's
Naval Brigade was now making. For weeks they had been reading the signals
exchanged between the Union fleet and the army headquarters on shore, thanks to
a code book discovered earlier aboard the wrecked *USS Keokuk*. The Rebels had
also noticed the boats gathering among the Union fleet earlier in the day.[18] As a
result, the assaulting troops quickly found themselves in an uncomfortable situation. The Confederates waited until the Union boats approached below the walls
and then, after they failed to respond to a hail from the fort, a signal rocket
pierced the darkness and announced the discovery of the Federal force to the
harbor's defenders. Firing broke out immediately. A number of the first division

managed to land at the base of the fort. In accordance with their orders, many of the marines on the scene began blazing away at the walls in an attempt to cover their comrades' progress. It was soon apparent, however, that the marines were endangering the exposed Union sailors far more than the Confederate defenders, and orders to "cease fire" were shouted from officers of the force which had already landed. The few who had successfully disembarked were already being subjected to a hail of grenades and loose masonry poured on them from the fort's defenders. To make matters worse, it appeared that there was no way for the attackers to enter the fort itself from their position. The expedition's trappings did not include scaling equipment.

The sailors and marines still in boats around the fort were rapidly degenerating into a panicked mob. Much of their understandable confusion came about because of a deadly fire from Fort Sumter as well as from Fort Moultrie, the Confederate ironclad *CSS Chicora*, and all of the harbor batteries that could make the range. When the orders to "cease fire" had gone up, first from the Union forces already landed and then echoed by several of the marine and navy officers still in boats, many of the launches not only stopped their firing, but turned around and headed back to the squadron with all possible speed. Much to the surprise of Captain McCawley, whose rear-echelon marines had not yet landed, the boat containing Cmdr. Thomas H. Stevens, the navy officer in command of the expedition, was leading the withdrawal.[19] The retreat soon became a general rout with the unfortunate result that many of those that had landed found themselves deserted with no option but to surrender.[20]

The assault on Fort Sumter was an embarrassing failure. More than 100 prisoners were taken by the Confederates, including about thirty marines. The army wisely aborted its own effort after witnessing the disaster that befell the Naval Brigade. Admiral Dahlgren in particular failed to appreciate that such a specialized task required a higher level of training than his men enjoyed. Two of the sailors captured during the expedition were sufficiently impressed by the outcome of the operation that "they took the oath of allegiance and (were) now in the Southern Confederacy."[21] At least one of the marine officers thought that Commander Stevens was drunk.[22] Most of the officers who survived the expedition believed that if the assault had been managed properly, and that if the men had been trained and experienced enough to avoid the panic and hesitation that crippled the operation, Fort Sumter could have been seized that night.[23] Despite the failure of the assault, the admiral commended the marines for their services, and all five Marine officers who survived received brevet promotions.[24]

Top Left: Lt. C. H. Bradford, mortally wounded in the boat attack on Fort Sumter; top right: Lt. Jones in full dress uniform, K.I.A. 1864 during bombardment of Fort Fisher; left: Lt. W. B. Breese in dress uniform, with unidentified female. Photos courtesy of the Marine Historical Center.

Soon after the disastrous assault on Sumter, Marine Lt. Col. John G. Reynolds arrived to take command of the battalion, owing to illness on the part of Major Zeilin. The marines moved to a luxurious camp on Folly Island, where, for all intents and purposes, they were shelved. The marine battalion was subsequently used as a replacement pool by the *Pawnee*, *Marblehead* and *C. P. Williams*, stationed off Folly Island, as well as other vessels of the squadron.

By late October only about 170 marines remained on duty due to illness and demands on the battalion's manpower. By the end of the year the battalion no longer existed; those who had not been sent back to Washington Barracks for reassignment were absorbed into the South Atlantic Blockading Squadron.[25] Like the other Marine battalions during the Civil War, which were all more or less extemporized, the Charleston battalion had not been intended as a permanent organization. Once the rationale for its existence disappeared, the commandant was anxious to have it back for the manpower it represented.[26]

*   *   *

The unhappy results of the Fort Sumter episode did not diminish Dahlgren's interest in naval field forces. In late 1864, the admiral formed a new Naval Brigade, alternately referred to as the "Fleet Brigade," to participate in operations intended to complement the march of Maj. Gen. William T. Sherman's armies from Atlanta to the sea. This new brigade was organized following a request for cooperation from Maj. Gen. John G. Foster, whose army forces were preparing for an expedition up the Broad River at Port Royal, South Carolina. Their goal was to sever the Charleston and Savannah Railroad, the main supply artery connecting Savannah to the remainder of the Confederacy to the north. The railroad passed to within a few miles of the proposed landing site of the joint expedition. Foster expected that the Rebel railroad defenses would be weakened by the withdrawal of troops to meet Sherman's advance and would therefore be particularly ripe for a successful attack.[27] The hastily assembled "Coast Division" numbered over 5,000 men: two army brigades, the Fleet Brigade and elements of three army batteries.[28] Unlike the admiral's previous brigade, this smaller formation was drawn entirely from within the South Atlantic Blockading Squadron.

The marine component of Admiral Dahlgren's second Naval Brigade was entrusted to 1st Lt. George G. Stoddard, who was detached from service aboard the *USS New Hampshire* for that purpose. Stoddard received word of his assignment on November 24, 1864, the same day that the admiral directed Capt. Joseph F. Green, senior officer of the Charleston blockade, to send all available marines from the vessels under his command to Port Royal; Dahlgren himself was already stripping the vessels off Port Royal of their own ships' guards. The Charleston marines were dispatched aboard the sidewheel gunboat *Pontiac* and headed for the assembly area at Bay Point on Phillip's Island, Port Royal Bay. Stoddard was charged with seeing that the marines were instructed in battalion drill and equipped for service in the field. A levy of "contrabands" was detailed to perform the cooking and fatigue duties of the assembling Fleet Brigade, so that they might not be distracted from their drill.[29] The marines were intended to make up one-third of the new brigade, a similar organizational framework to Dahlgren's previous formation.[30] They were to fill the role of infantry, while one battalion of "sailor infantry" operated as skirmishers and another formed an artillery component. This artillery unit was made up largely of sailors drawn from the naval battery at Morris Island, since Dahlgren lacked experienced men at Port Royal. Command of the brigade devolved onto Cmdr. George H. Preble, USN, a veteran of almost thirty years in the service. Preble hoped to redeem his reputation in this expedition, since it remained tarnished after he had allowed the Confederate raider *CSS Florida* to run the blockade at Mobile in late 1862.[31]

The admiral stressed to his battalion commanders that the drill utilized should be as simple as possible, indicating that "the evolutions (should) be simply from the order of march to action, and the reverse." It was expected, therefore, that the marines would operate in skirmish order and would in battle protect the two four-gun batteries of naval howitzers. With an anticipated date of movement four days from the organization's inception, accomplishment of even this limited a command of battlefield maneuver was difficult. Lieutenant Stoddard's task was not made any easier by the fact that he was the only marine officer assigned to the brigade. Indeed, he was the only marine officer in the squadron at that time. The other officers with the marine battalion were Acting Ensign Woodward Carter, like Stoddard detached from the *New Hampshire*, and admiral's clerk J. R. Stanley, who served as battalion adjutant. A marine sergeant filled the role of captain for each small company. Since the last of the ships' guards did not arrive at the Bay Point assembly area until the evening of November 27, Stoddard's 157-man battalion did not get to begin practicing their drill evolutions until the 28th. That very evening they embarked on the *USS Sonoma* for the trip up the Broad River.[32]

Some of the expedition's vessels went up the wrong river, some grounded, and it was the Naval Brigade that first arrived intact at the landing site. Stoddard had divided his command into three lettered companies (A, B and C). At daylight on November 29, Company A went ashore in ship's boats at Boyd's Landing, on

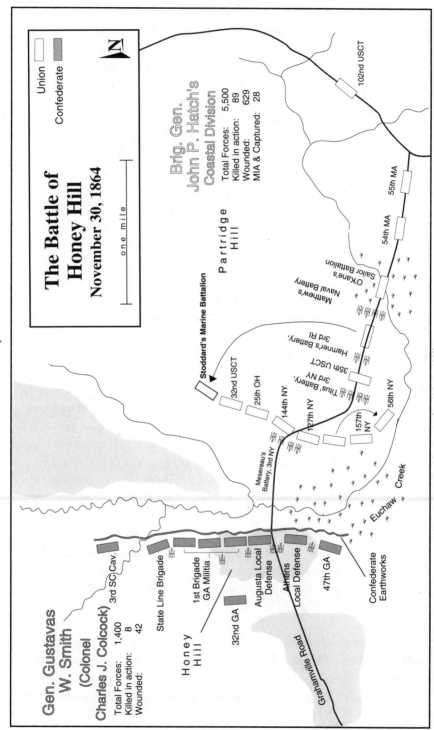

The Battle of Honey Hill
November 30, 1864

one mile

Union
Confederate

N

Brig. Gen. John P. Hatch's Coastal Division

Total Forces:	5,500
Killed in action:	89
Wounded:	629
MIA & Captured:	28

102nd USCT

55th MA

54th MA

O'Kane's Sailor Battalion

Matthew's Naval Battery

Hammer's Battery, 3rd RI

35th USCT

Trius' Battery, 3rd NY

Partridge Hill

Stoddard's Marine Battalion

32nd USCT

25th OH

144th NY

127th NY

157th NY

56th NY

Mesereau's Battery, 3rd NY

Euchaw Creek

Gen. Gustavas W. Smith
(Colonel Charles J. Colcock)

Total Forces:	1,400
Killed in action:	8
Wounded:	42

3rd SC Cav.

State Line Brigade

1st Brigade GA Militia

Honey Hill

32nd GA

Augusta Local Defense

Athens Local Defense

47th GA

Confederate Earthworks

Grahamville Road

Map by David A. Woodbury. Adapted in part from William Scaife's *The March to the Sea*, (Atlanta, 1989).

Boyd's Creek, off the Broad River. The other elements of the Naval Brigade, which numbered just under 500 men, soon followed, and at 7:30 a.m. the marines began their advance, driving back Rebel pickets along the way. When the Boyd's Landing Road reached a dead end at the Coosawhatchie-Savannah Road, Preble chose to follow the right hand route, thereby taking the Naval Brigade north and away from the Grahamville Road, which was his objective. The brigade marched three miles before realizing the error, and was compelled to counter march four miles before at last reaching the Grahamville Road. By this time it had joined up with the army contingent of the expedition under the command of Brig. Gen. John P. Hatch. The counter-marching was especially hard on the naval batteries, which, aided by the "sailor infantry," were obliged to haul their own guns with tow-ropes since they lacked the requisite horses. While the tired Naval Brigade rested, the army column continued on; unfortunately, they too took a wrong road and returned to their starting point. The next morning, November 30, the advance on the Charleston and Savannah Railroad began again, minus two of the lightest howitzers from the naval batteries, which had been detached in order to stay behind and guard the Union rear. The Naval Brigade was posted in the rear of the Union line of march.

The Federal troops had advanced no more than five or six miles when they collided with squadrons of Col. Charles J. Colcock's 3rd South Carolina Cavalry and mixed units of Georgia Militia under Gen. Gustavus W. Smith. Smith's Georgians, veterans of the fighting at Griswoldville, had just arrived the night before on the Charleston and Savannah Railroad after being rerouted from Savannah by Maj. Gen. William J. Hardee. At about 9:15 a.m., the first artillery shell exploded among the advancing Federals, precipitating the Battle of Honey Hill. The Union column pushed back the advanced Confederate detachments for over three miles, until it developed the main Rebel line at about 11:00 a.m. Through Colcock's delaying actions, the Confederates were able to complete a mile-long line of rifle-pits and trenches, bolstered by artillery redoubts on either side of the Grahamville Road. Facing a continuous storm of musketry fire and inhospitable terrain, the Federals were unable to close with the Confederate line, and in the seeming absence of any tactical battle plans from General Hatch, the Union assault remained sporadic and fragmented all along the front.

The marines were initially kept in reserve, but about two hours into the engagement Stoddard's battalion was ordered forward along with the 55th Massachusetts, relieving the 144th New York on the right of the Union line. The marines advanced slowly through nearly a mile of thick woods and swamp before going into line of battle on the double-quick. After this formation change, they exchanged fire with Confederate infantry and artillery for about three hours. The battalion's acting quartermaster-sergeant, J. Cogley, braved heavy Confederate fire to keep his marines supplied with ammunition from the rear. Around 2:00 p.m., Ensign Carter took 20 marines and attempted to feel out the Confederate left flank. Unfortunately, after moving some 200 yards without finding the flank, and likely feeling uncomfortable about his separation from the main line, Carter led his detachment back to its starting point. Stoddard's marines could see only a small portion of the battlefield, but it was evident that the attempt to push through to the railroad was proving unsuccessful. Unable to break through the entrenched Confederates, the marines withdrew with the rest of the Federal troops that evening.

Stoddard's battalion helped cover the withdrawal and established itself near its original position, where the marines prepared defenses and performed picket duty. Despite the length of the engagement at Honey Hill, the day's fighting had left but one marine killed, six wounded and one missing.[33] The marines were posted on the left of the naval batteries, whose march to and from the Honey Hill battlefield had been eased by the charitable loan of some artillery horses from the army. For the next few days Stoddard took advantage of the lull to drill his marines. They had performed better than reasonably could have been expected during the fighting at Honey Hill, and the opportunity for drill could serve only to enhance their unit cohesion and ability to function creditably in battle.

Rebuffed in the attempt to break the railroad, Admiral Dahlgren and General Foster decided to try a different approach. Late on the night of December 5, the Naval Brigade set off for its embarkation point once more, this time to board the flag-steamer *Philadelphia* for another assault against the railroad. The latest attempt would be launched further north by way of the Tullifinny River. Lieutenant Stoddard had managed to squeeze in just three days of drill between the actions. This time Brig. Gen. Edward E. Potter's 1st Brigade landed first and moved inland toward the Charleston & Savannah Railroad bridge across the Tullifinny River. The Federals quickly came into contact with a motley assemblage of Confederate state militia and South Carolina military academy cadets, but once again failed to punch through to their objective.[34] The marines, advancing on the right of the naval batteries, did not come under fire until about 11:00 a.m., two hours after the Battle of Tullifinny Crossroads had begun. The Naval Brigade had been unavoidably delayed when their landing site turned out to be tangled and marshy, requiring construction of a temporary log road to move the howitzers.

The marines were shifted about from one flank to the other during the day's engagement, finally ending up in support of an army battery in the center. Company C was under Acting Ensign Carter, on whom Stoddard conferred the dignity of "acting major" of marines while serving with the battalion, and was on picket during the night at the extreme left of the Union line, away from the rest of the battalion. The marines had left behind their blankets and overcoats before entering battle, and that night they slept in the open under a heavy rain.

At daylight the next morning the Confederates counterattacked, driving back the troops on Company C's right, effectively cutting them off from the rest of the Federal force. Carter's marines maintained their discipline and organization, however, and he managed to extricate them from their uncomfortable position with the loss of only one man wounded. The Confederate assault sputtered out about midday, and the Union troops fell to fortifying their position and preparing to make another assault on the Rebels on December 9. On December 8 the battalion, which had lost almost a dozen of its number since setting out, received a welcome reinforcement of twenty-five men from the ships' guards of the *Cimarron* and the *Donegal*. They had been forwarded by the admiral once the losses from the Honey Hill battle had become known.[35]

The next day, in the third attempt to sever the railroad, the Federals again attacked at the Tullifinny River bridge, and later at nearby Coosawhatchie. The marines occupied the extreme right of the 600-man Federal "skirmish brigade." The renewed assault began at about 9:00 a.m., with the objective of clearing 100-foot wide lines of fire through the woods to allow Union artillery to shell the railroad, since it seemed impossible to break through the Confederate defenses. Stoddard's battalion was posted on the right of the line, the men in one rank and about two paces apart. Advancing against the Confederate position, the marines trudged doggedly through tangled swamp that was in some places waist-deep. The skirmish line was supported by another 1,000 Union troops, which, in turn, were followed by the ax-wielding 25th Ohio, felling trees to form the required lines of fire. Stoddard's battalion successfully advanced to within fifty yards of the Confederate defenders in an attempt to charge a Confederate battery, but it became entangled in a dense thicket and pulled back under a heavy shelling. When the order for the skirmishers to withdraw was given shortly thereafter, the marines did not receive it. The lieutenant, in fact, had been contemplating charging the Rebel lines once again, but with the retreat of the troops on their left, the marines found themselves isolated.[36] The Confederates surged forward to pursue the withdrawing Federal line, and Stoddard pulled back and tried to extricate his endangered battalion.

In this instance, at least, the dense swamp served Stoddard's marines well, as they eluded Confederate pursuit and made their way back to the Tullifinny River.

From there, Stoddard slipped his battalion through Southern units looking for Union stragglers and at last made his way back to the original position. The heavy skirmishing continued, however, and the marines were assigned a new post on the Federal left. The Fleet Brigade helped to repel Rebel counterattacks throughout the afternoon while the work of cutting the fire lanes was being carried out. It was now the Confederates' turn to assault through the wooded swampland, and they were no more successful than the exhausted Union troops had been. The Federal forces found the new objective of setting up artillery positions to bombard the railroad to be a more manageable task. After cutting the woods to permit a sufficient field of fire, they withdrew to their artillery positions at about 3:00 p.m., while beating off Rebel attacks until shortly after dark.[37]

Thereafter, the operation took on the aspect of a stalemate, with the Confederate forces too weak to repulse the entrenched Federals and with the Federal forces too small to break through the Rebel defenders. There was to be no more serious fighting. The Federal troops established a number of batteries at varying ranges from the railroad in what were essentially siege operations. The marines provided support for the naval batteries when they participated several times in shelling the railroad , but most of their time was spent in duties about camp and in drill.[38]

Foster was not pleased when the expedition sputtered to a halt. The goal had been to "prepare for the arrival of General Sherman," and with that officer's seizure of Savannah on December 21, coupled with the persistent heavy rains that inhibited operations, the continued presence of the Naval Brigade and its army associates was no longer a priority. On December 27, the Naval Brigade was transported to Bay Point, arriving on the morning of December 28.[39] The sailor elements of the brigade were dispersed to their respective vessels, while the marines went into camp. On January 5, 1865, the Marine battalion was finally disbanded, the ship's guards returning to their posts.

Stoddard's battalion had lost 23 killed, wounded and missing during their six weeks of service. Admiral Dahlgren had described the Naval Brigade as being, upon its departure for battle, "as carefully drilled as the brief space of time allowed." Considering that the marines' battalion drill was the work of a single afternoon, and that the entire force was made up of tiny detachments from a dozen vessels throughout the South Atlantic Blockading Squadron, its members performed far better than anyone had a right to expect. This is to say nothing of the fact that only one Marine officer, a junior lieutenant filling a field-grade command, was with the battalion throughout its operations. Both the admiral's clerk Stanley, who missed the Tullifinny Crossroads battles on account of illness, and especially Acting Ensign Carter, performed creditably. Preble's acting adjutant, Lt.-Cmdr. A. F. Crosman, joined the marines during both battles as a volunteer so as not to impinge upon Stoddard's authority, who was his junior in rank. Still, the marines earned the approval of the admiral for their good work, and Stoddard received a captain's brevet for his services.[40]

The Broad River expedition represented the last Marine field operation of any size within the area of the South Atlantic Blockading Squadron. The focus of coastal action moved northward with Sherman's armies, and many of the marines who had gained experience by their participation in Admiral Dahlgren's Naval Brigades would go on to serve with the ill-fated naval column in the bloody assault on Fort Fisher, North Carolina in early 1865.

Notes

1. *The Official Records of the Union and Confederate Navies in the War of the Rebellion* (Washington, D.C., 1894-1927), 30 vols., ser. I, vol. 14, pp. 337, 340, hereinafter cited as *ORN*. All references are to series I unless otherwise specified.

2. Ibid., pp. 386-387.

3. Ibid., pp. 395, 401, 404.

4. Jacob Zeilin Biographical File, Historical Division, Headquarters, U. S. Marine Corps, hereinafter cited as *HQMC*; Karl Schuon, *U.S. Marine Corps Biographical Dictionary* (New York, 1963), pp. 249-250; Col. John Harris to Maj. Jacob Zeilin, July 24, 1863, "Letters Sent, 1798-1884," Record Group 127, National Archives, hereinafter cited as NA.

5. Colonel John Harris to Gideon Welles, July 31, 1863, "Letters Sent, 1798-1884," NA.

6. Frederick Tomlinson Peet, *Personal Experiences in the Civil War* (New York: fifty copies- privately printed, 1905), pp. 77-78.

7. *ORN* 14, pp. 420, 428.

8. Ibid., p. 428.

9. Peet, *Personal Experiences*, p. 80.

10. *ORN* 14, p. 434.

11. Ibid., pp. 428-429; It seems that the crossbelts of the marine guards from the *New Ironsides, South Carolina* and *Wabash*, at least, were dyed black by the sanction of the admiral. See Captain Edward McD. Reynolds to Colonel John Harris, August 17, 1863,

quoted in Richard A. Long, "Send Me Thirty Marines," *Leatherneck*, Vol. 44, No. 5 (May, 1961), p. 50.

12. Fort Sumter had suffered a severe enough pounding during the Federal siege to render it unimportant as an artillery post, but the fort and its garrison continued to serve as the anchor for the torpedoes and sea lane obstructions that barred Union access to Charleston Harbor.

13. *ORN* 14., pp. 439-440.

14. Ibid., p. 539.

15. McCawley eventually ascended to the Marines' highest office, serving as commandant from 1876 to 1891. The battalion's original commander, Maj. Jacob Zeilin, succeeded Col. John Harris as commandant upon the latter's death in 1864.

16. Johnson, Robert W., and Clarence C. Buel, eds., *Battles and Leaders of the Civil War*, 4 vols. (New York, 1887-1888), vol. 4, p. 49.

17. *ORN* 14, pp. 623-624.

18. Rowena Reed, *Combined Operations of the Civil War* (Annapolis, 1978), p. 312. The *Keokuk* was a casualty of Du Pont's earlier ironclad assault on the fort. Along with the code book, the ship's guns had been salvaged and were installed by the Confederates in the Charleston defenses, a circumstance that greatly irritated Secretary Welles.

19. In Stevens' defense, it may be noted that he had been given command of the expedition on the very day it was expected to go into action. He later claimed that the whole plan of operation went against his better judgment. Johnson and Buel, *Battles and Leaders*, pp. 47-51.

20. *ORN* 14, pp. 622-630, 636-637; U. S. War Department, *The War of the Rebellion: The Official Records of the Union and Confederate Armies,*128 vols. (Washington, D.C., 1890-1901), series I, vol. 28, pt. 1, pp. 724-728.

21. *ORN* 14, p. 630.

22. Lt. F. T. Peet to his Father, Sept. 9, 1863, quoted in *Civil War Letters and Documents of Frederick Tomlinson Peet* (Newport: fifty copies- privately printed, 1905), pp. 247-248.

23. *ORN* 14, pp. 622-630.

24. Lieutenant C. H. Bradford, the battalion's quartermaster, was mortally wounded and captured the night of the assault.

25. *ORN* 15, pp. 9, 71; Peet, *Personal Experiences*, pp. 86-88; Richard S. Collum, *History of the United States Marine Corps* (New York, 1903), pp. 154-159.

26. *ORN* 25, pp. 590-591.

27. *OR* 44, p. 525.

28. Ibid., pp. 421-425.

29. Ibid., pp. 421-425.

30. Ibid., pp. 67, 72, 74.

31. Ibid., p. 66; Edward W. Callahan, *List of Officers of the Navy of the United States and of the Marine Corps, 1775-1900* (New York, 1901), p. 445.

32. *ORN* 16, p. 67 (first quotation), p. 99.

33. Most of the Naval Brigade's casualties were marines. Total Federal casualties at Honey Hill numbered 746, including 89 killed. *OR* 44, pp. 421-425. See map on page 207 for Union and Confederate Orders of Battle at Honey Hill.

34. The Confederates at Tullifinny Crossroads (December 6-9, 1864), were under the overall command of District Commander Maj. Gen. Samuel Jones. Though records are incomplete, those units engaged primarily included the 5th and 47th GA., a battalion of the 32nd GA., the 1st and 3rd GA. Reserves, a company of the 1st SC Artillery, a battalion of SC military cadets, one company of the 1st SC infantry with numerous SC militia, the 7th NC Reserves, the Augusta Battalion (local defense troops) and Bachman's Charleston (SC) Battery. *OR* 44, pp. 438-448.

35. *ORN* 16, p. 86.

36. Stoddard behaved with remarkable courage during the advance on the Confederate line, a fact attested to by his army colleagues in the engagement. *OR* 44, pp. 438-448.

37. Ibid.; *ORN* 16, pp. 99-102, 104-108.

38. At this point Admiral Dahlgren began to fear that prolonged contact with volunteer army troops might corrupt his sailors and marines, eroding what he termed "the more exact and respectful training of the Navy." He warned Commander Preble accordingly. Ibid., p. 88.

39. In Dahlgren's opinion, Preble withdrew the brigade somewhat hastily. The admiral felt that the brigade should not have been embarked until the army had a given a clear indication that its services were no longer necessary. Ibid., pp. 94-96.

40. By late February 1865, Stoddard commanded seven companies of marines at Georgetown, SC.

Classic Regimental Book Shelf
An Interview With Author William C. Davis

The Orphan Brigade: The Kentucky Confederates Who Couldn't Go Home
(New York, 1980). Photos, , biblio., index. 318pp.

David A. Lang

DAL: How did you come to write about the Orphan Brigade?

WCD: It was an outgrowth of the biography I did of John C. Breckinridge, the Orphan Brigade's first commander in the war and the one they stayed most attached to during the course of the war. Doing the research and then the writing on Breckinridge, I became very interested in them as a body of men themselves. Most of my books are an outgrowth of a previous book.

DAL: The Orphan Brigade won its fame by its performance in battle. And yet, doesn't the romantic name "Orphan Brigade" help in a small way to sustain that fame—somewhat like the "Lost Battalion" of World War I?

WCD: Sure. The brigades that are best known from the Civil War are the ones that had some kind of a nickname and not just a number: The Laurel Brigade, The Excelsior Brigade, The Stonewall Brigade.

DAL: The Iron Brigade. . .

WCD: Yes, The Iron Brigade—of the west. You know, there were two Iron Brigades.

DAL: *The question is not meant to be a reflection at all on the gallantry of the Orphan Brigade, merely a comment on the way we remember the past.*

WCD: Well, the famous brigades weren't necessarily in all cases the most proficient or the most hard-fighting brigades. Generally the nicknames had something to do with a personality or a style or a flair—something that set them apart. In some it cases it *was* fighting like the Stonewall Brigade and their association with Jackson. In the case of the Orphan Brigade, it was so uniquely fitting to them because they spent the whole war as orphans from their native state. They could not go home. They were literally orphans of the storm. Hey, someone should do a movie with that title.

DAL: *Many members of the brigade showed a natural hesitancy in their decision to fight for the Confederacy. Did any later express regret over the decision?*

WCD: I'm not aware of any who expressed regret after the war. A lot of them expressed regret over the *war* of course. Like most Confederates, having made the decision, they wouldn't have been human if they had been able to just ignore the impulse to justify their actions. The one who came closet I suppose was Breckinridge himself. There's no question: He never wanted the war; he never wanted succession; he never wanted to be a Confederate. He was essentially forced out of the Union in part by his beliefs and in part by his arrest being ordered when he hadn't done anything. So his choices were to go to war, be a political prisoner in a Yankee prison, or go South. But soon after the war, he made a statement that the the country was much better being reunited.

DAL: *Was there a significant difference in the discipline or training of the brigade's regiments?*

WCD: As near as I can judge, the best drilled and disciplined units were the 2nd and the 4th Kentuckians. The 2nd was Colonel Roger Hanson's regiment. Hanson, of course, was a Mexican War veteran and a real stickler for order. Those two were probably the best, and that's pretty much typical of most Civil War units, by the way. The ones with the lower numbers of course are the first ones raised. They usually have the best troops because they are all volunteer and they have the longest time to get drilled before they get thrown into action. And of course they have the most battle experience. They're the ones who also get eaten up by the end of the war, but they're usually the ones who do better in drill. I think the 2nd and the 6th were the ones who won most of the drill competitions.

DAL: Did any of the men of the Orphan Brigade ever have any inkling that Breckinridge had grave doubts about the Confederacy's ability to win the war?

WCD: I'm sure he would have kept that sort of thing to himself. I've never found anything to indicate that, and in fact, other than a few young men who served on his staff and a couple of the top officers, Breckinridge was not that close personally to many of the Orphans. He felt great affection for them, and they for him, but they weren't in his close circle of pre-war associates that he tended to confide in.

DAL: At one point the Orphan Brigade mutinied, refusing to reenlist and continue fighting the war. Was this mutiny unique on a Brigade level?

WCD: No. I can't immediately think of any other Confederate units that did this although I'm sure there were some. There were a couple of mutinies in the Yankee army on the regimental level. I think the 3rd Pennsylvania Calvary—reputed to be the absolute worst regiment in the Civil War—and there were others who just sort of laid down their arms and refused to serve. At First Manassas, some of the ninety-day regiments whose enlistments expired July 20, 1861, refused to fight. They said, in effect, "We don't care if you're about to fight the battle. We've done enough."

DAL: Did later reunions of the Orphan Brigade tend to gloss over the mutinies?

WCD: You don't find much about it. I don't think you find anything about it in the first unit histories—Ed Porter Thomasson's *History of the First Kentucky Brigade* in 1868, for example. I don't think it's mentioned at all there. It *is* dealt with in an anecdote in his 1898 version [*History of the Orphan Brigade*]. Of the few published memoirs, a couple do mention it, a couple don't. There are only a few genuine Orphan Brigade diaries, and they mention it, but they give somewhat varying stories.

DAL: Was it considered impolite to mention it?

WCD: I don't think they were particularly proud of it immediately afterwards. You get two versions of how the mutiny ended: The popular version that appealed to the Orphans was that somebody made a patriotic speech—probably Breckinridge—and a few of the boys yelled "Huzzah! Huzzah! We'll fight for you until the end of the war, until the end of time" and, as one man, they all stepped forward and reenlisted. The other version which survives in a diary written at the time is that Breckinridge came out and said "I will either have unconditional surrender or unconditional mutiny" and gave them ten minutes to get back in the ranks or else. He didn't say what that "else" was, but that story has the ring of truth about it. Memory over the generations changed the mutiny into, "Well, we weren't really serious about it. We were just making our point. It was like a strike."

DAL: Why were there are so few diaries from the Orphan Brigade?

WCD: I can't account for it. In fact, it's an anomaly, a mystery. Man for man, they were probably among the half dozen best educated, most literate brigades in the Confederate army. I couldn't make a guess as to what percentage of literacy they had, but it was high because Kentuckians were fairly literate people for that time. I've only been able to find one string of letters written by a member of the brigade. You can understand that because home was behind Yankee lines, so any letter they wrote had to go through a flag of truce, through a whole lot of hassle. And the Orphan Brigade moved around as much if not more than almost any other Confederate unit in the Army of Tennessee. So it may have been just a logistical impracticability for them to correspond. But why there are no diaries is a hell of a mystery to me. There's the so-called "Johnny Green of the Orphan Brigade" which is not a diary at all. It is chiefly post-war reminiscences and a lot of stuff that is lifted from the genuine diary of John Jackman, which is in the Library of Congress and is the only full time war diary there is. I edited it and published it several years ago. There is a small diary by a fellow named Squire Helm Bush that only covers, oh, not more than a year or two years of the war. And I found a diary by Lieutenant Colonel John Caldwell, which covers the first year of the war, and he was Lieutenant Colonel of the 6th, later the 9th

Kentucky. It's a very good, full diary but unfortunately it ends shortly after Shiloh. I ran ads in every county seat in central and eastern Kentucky that contributed companies to the Orphan Brigade advertising for diaries and letters. I only had one response, and that was from someone who didn't really have anything. Everything else I just found.

DAL: It must have been particularly galling to the Orphan Brigade to have Hanson ordered to supervise the execution of one of their own, Asa Lewis. And Braxton Bragg, who—shockingly—doesn't come off too well in this whole business [laughter] was absolutely unwilling to grant a pardon to Lewis. I have always been curious whether Breckinridge ever harbored suspicions that it was Bragg's dislike of him personally and the Kentuckians in general which made Bragg unwilling to grant the pardon?

WCD: Everybody else suspected it. I don't recall Breckinridge himself ever making any reference indicating there was something like that in it. A lot of the Orphans themselves thought that Bragg had an antipathy to Kentuckians in general because Kentucky—as Bragg saw it—had let him down in the Kentucky campaign and then he transferred a lot of that antipathy to Breckinridge in particular because Breckinridge didn't get his command to Bragg's army in time. Therefore the failure of the Kentucky campaign was Breckinridge's fault because if he had been with Bragg, Kentuckians would have rallied by the tens of thousands to Breckinridge. This was purely a figment of Bragg's imagination—the Kentuckians simply didn't want to be in the Confederate army. But I don't know that Breckinridge ever stated that Bragg's dislike of the Kentuckians had something to do with his failure to pardon Lewis. Some of Breckinridge's family certainly felt that way.

DAL: There's one little detail that struck me: Why didn't Breckinridge return Lewis' personal items to his family until 1869?

WCD: I can only guess. He probably didn't know where Lewis' mother—well wait, Lewis would have told Breckinridge where his mother lived. But then again, there was no way getting stuff through the lines safely until the war was over, but it says more that he kept the stuff as long as he did. Interesting point here: Asa's mother, Sally Lewis, sent Breckinridge a thank-you letter. About six or seven years ago, I got a letter from Sally Lewis' granddaughter, and I was able to send her a copy of the thank-you letter written by Sally Lewis to Breckinridge. The granddaughter had never known about it.

DAL: The fact that the Orphans did not cheer Bragg when he and President Davis reviewed the troops at Chattanooga is telling. I wonder what effect that had on Davis at that moment, what thoughts were going through his mind. Here he is with one of his leading generals, they're riding by brigade after brigade, Bragg is getting cheered—somewhat perfunctorily, but he is getting cheered—and they get to the regiments of the Orphan Brigade and there's not a sound out of any of them.

WCD: Actually one letter turned up and Bob Krick's son sent this to me a few years ago. It's a letter by a Kentucky soldier in the Orphan Brigade, and it describes that incident. It's my recollection from this letter that he says that some men did cheer. I don't believe he indicated that it was the same kind of rousing huzzah! huzzah! that there was all along the rest of the line but only that at least some men around him did cheer. It's possible that the snub to Bragg is part of Orphan Brigade lore: we couldn't shoot him but we refused to cheer him. So they might have exaggerated what was a luke warm response into a hostile response. As far as what was going through Davis' mind, Davis already knew that he was dealing with an army that already had a poisoned culture in its headquarters. And that was pretty much spreading through the army, so if he observed that, it probably only endeared Bragg to him [laughs].

DAL: What do you think was the high point of the war for the Orphan Brigade on the battlefield?

WCD: Hmm, I've never thought about it really, but I guess I'd say Chickamauga because along with another brigade—Cleburne's—they kicked the living hell out of George Thomas. He was the "Rock of Chickamauga" later on, but he had feet of clay at that point. The Confederates scared the hell out of him, causing him to send these repeated, panicked reports back to Rosecrans: "Send me more men. I'm outflanked and outnumbered" —which he was not. He had numerical superiority, but they just pounded him into thinking that he was, indeed, getting beat. I'd be inclined to say that was probably their best moment.

DAL: Who was the best, most effective, commander of the Orphan Brigade?

WCD: [Pause] Nobody commanded it for more than one battle.

DAL: Right, and that's what makes this a hard question.

WCD: Well, Breckinridge never personally lead them in battle. At Shiloh he was already at corps command. I guess you'd have to say Joseph Lewis, simply because he commands them for the last year and a half of the war—although by that point they're a shadow of what they were beforehand, but it's Lewis who keeps them together, who helps keep their morale high. And they *are* good in the Atlanta campaign and they're fighting under Lewis, so I guess I'd have to say him. He's the least colorful of all the commanders and the one the Orphans are the least attached to, I think. They really liked Helm, and they liked Breckinridge. They liked Hanson too, because he was sort of their Stonewall Jackson, with all his peculiarities.

DAL: Did Lewis leave much in the way of writings after the war?

WCD: I located a great granddaughter of his. She had no papers whatever. It's been so long ago I don't recall, but it may have been the old story of a house fire. She had a printed copy of his farewell address to his troops, and she had a scrapbook of his that had mostly post-war clippings about him and about the brigade. But I don't recall that she had anything else.

DAL: He never wrote anything that was published? No articles?

WCD: No, he didn't write any articles. None of them did. Breckinridge never wrote anything about the brigade after the war. Their story is told primarily by some lower level officers. Ed Porter Thompson and Basil Duke, who wasn't even a member of the brigade, are two of the key people who preserved the history of the Orphans. The Orphan Brigade history comes from the low-level field officer perspective.

DAL: How do you think that source, coming from such a narrow slice of the brigade, affects our perception of the unit?

WCD: That's an interesting question but I confess I never thought of it while writing the book. But it must have affected it. Other than the reports that are published in the Official Records, the view from headquarters doesn't survive. None of the people who are writing in the *Southern Bivouac* and elsewhere were on staff. At the same time, these are all literate, middle or upper-middle class men for their time. It's a good point: we may have a slightly upper middle class view of things. Probably the best overall representations available are in the Ed Porter Thompson's books, which I think are two model brigade histories. In his first volume, he's actually researching while the war's going on. He printed circulars to solicit recollections from the Orphans; he was very well organized. In his second volume he interviewed so many people and gathered their recollections, especially at the reunions, that you do get some worm's-eye-view stuff there. But you never get anything from the brigade commanders.

DAL: One of the Orphan Brigade's key roles in the war was covering retreats. Do you think that role affected the brigade's morale? Did it waste their talents?

WCD: No, not really. If only because a unit that becomes noted for any particular role begins to feel a certain pride and elan which only makes them more effective in that role. That's not to say the Orphans wouldn't have been the best troops at something else, but they were very good at covering retreats. And the rear guard is pretty important for an army that spends a lot of time retreating [laughter].

DAL: Apparently the Orphan Brigade was tense and nervous on the retreat from Vicksburg retreat in 1863. This is uncharacteristic for men who had performed well in other retreats. Was there a particularly strong psychological blow in the loss of Vicksburg that made them falter on this retreat? Were they just plain worn out from the horrendous field conditions?

WCD: Well for one thing, I think they were not at all keen about the fact that in leaving Vicksburg, they were on their way back to Braxton Bragg because they loathed Bragg. And they had had a bad experience the year before with the hot, malarial summer, and here they were getting another dose. The fall of Vicksburg had to be demoralizing because they had thought they would get there in time. Now I don't recall any statement to this effect, but I have to tell you that if I were in any army commanded by Joseph E. Johnston, my morale would be low [laughs]. But the war just had to be getting them down by this point.

DAL: Was there ever a moment in the war when the Orphans lost their heads and fled in panic?

WCD: Sure. Like virtually everyone else on Missionary Ridge, they skidaddled pretty good. And it bugged them that they lost their battery or a good part of their battery.

DAL: You tell a lot of stories about their colorful plundering of civilian foodstuffs, and so on. Did anyone after the war ever voice disenchantment with the Orphans for that?" Would such a complaint have been considered less than patriotic?

WCD: I've never encountered anyone complaining about it after the war, but my guess is that Confederate civilians "closed ranks" just the way the Confederate veterans did, and so they didn't want to admit publicly that their boys had behaved in any way that was less than exemplary. Besides, virtually every brigade in the war, Yankee and Confederate, given the opportunity, engaged in that sort of thing.

DAL: The Southerners held out the hope that an army campaigning in Kentucky could rally support for the Confederacy within that state. Yet you describe that support—and alluded to it earlier in this interview—as being in many ways "mythical." After the war, internecine bitterness lasted far longer there, it seems, than in any other state. Did the South ever really have much of a chance to rally support in Kentucky?

WCD: No. It was never in Kentuckians' interests to side whole heartedly with the Confederacy because Kentucky, thanks to the Ohio River, was tied too heavily commercially to the North. There were deep blood ties with the North as well as with the South. Kentucky had never been a hotbed of secession. Kentucky was the home of Henry Clay, and the ethic of "Henry Clay the Compromiser" was a part of the Kentuckian creed. So, most Kentuckians who went South did so reluctantly. The trouble was that too many of them misread things in one sense: they should have realized from their own reluctance to take the step that others back home would have been equally reluctant, if not more so. I'm currently editing what is the largest Confederate diary I've ever seen—a 2,000 page type-written transcript by a Kentucky cavalryman who's not in the Orphan Brigade, but with John Morgan. And what you see in his diary is one

long story of hope and then disillusionment with Kentucky's performance be-
cause he was all for the Confederacy, and he kept having his heart broken when
Kentucky didn't follow along. But no, I don't think there was ever a chance of
Kentucky going for the Confederacy.

DAL: Thanks Mr. Davis. We appreciate it.

WCD: My pleasure.

Book Reviews

Davis and Lee at War, by Steven E. Woodworth (University Press of Kansas, 2501 West 15th St., Lawrence, KS 66049-3904), 1995. Illus.,notes, biblio., maps, index. 409pp. HC. $29.95

"Superboy" Steve Woodworth has come through again and produced an absolutely splendid book, the second Eastern-oriented companion volume to pair with his *Jefferson Davis and His Generals: The Failure of Confederate Command in the West* (1990). In the almost one half-century since T. Harry Williams produced *Lincoln and His Generals*, many historians have toyed with concepts for the logical Confederate-oriented opposite study. Woodworth has achieved an offering without peer. This is a superb, insightful and stimulating quasi-biographical analysis of top-level military management, in some respects superior as biography (at least to the limited and qualified degree that it is proper to call this book biographical in nature) than any of the extant biographies of Lee or Davis.

Woodworth's main thesis is that Jefferson Davis and his most prominent general, Robert E. Lee, espoused fundamentally different ideas concerning the best options for Confederate grand strategy. Davis wanted a primarily defensive effort (despite his own self-named "offensive-defensive") that would be aimed first and foremost at ultimate Confederate survival. Lee, however, wanted an all-out effort to terminate the war with decisive battle. "Davis and [Joseph E.] Johnston," Woodworth states, "were inclined to await the enemy's movement and react accordingly, but Lee always preferred to take the initiative himself. Most important, Davis and especially Johnston thought primarily in terms of avoiding defeat, while Lee sought victory and hoped to make it complete. . .for Davis, the war could be won simply by not losing, for Lee, who never appeared to share his commander-in-chief's unquestioning confidence in the rightness or the ultimate success of the cause, it could be lost simply by not winning" (p. 157). "Davis would sacrifice as few lives as possible on each occasion until victory came," continues the author. "Lee would sacrifice as many lives as necessary in order to bring victory" (p. 215). Davis failed to make his preferences sufficiently clear and to state them with adequate authority and force; Lee, playing his cards as the master bridge player he would have been had he taken up that game, was not entirely candid and blunt with Davis concerning his intentions.

Woodworth is both critical and complimentary toward Davis, and so while pointing out numerous failures, flaws and shortcomings, his final assessment is a kind one. Indeed, Woodworth concludes, "Davis was the best the South could offer," and ". . . he was close to possessing. . . military genius. . . ." (p. 333). Assuredly the Confederate president had many faults and made some highly questionable decisions as a war leader; but he measured up better than most of his critics have asserted or opined, scholarly and lay people alike—in Davis' own time and off and on ever since. Woodworth, on the other hand, is also kind to Lee, and that may be the most serious flaw with Woodworth's scholarly assessment in toto herein, for in many respects Woodworth seems to be a disciple of Thomas L. Connelly—at least in regards to Connelly's assertion that Lee was too costly a general for the Confederacy to afford. Yet in the end Woodworth suggests that "Davis' choice of Robert E. Lee to succeed the fallen [Joseph E.] Johnston was his best of the war. Indeed, it probably deserves to be ranked with the few most brilliant command decisions of military history" (p. 329). In other words, I am suggesting that Woodworth in the end wants to "have his cake and eat it too." As a general Lee was quintessence; Davis was admirably acceptable as a commander in chief: But their strategic ideas were incompatible! The Confederate hope, like Davis himself, is thus rendered tragic.

Woodworth also fails to do much in the way of analyzing one of the main arguments in *How the North Won*—to whit, that not replacing Lee and his staff in Richmond when they took to the field was an egregious loss of potential administrative modernity that could have offered the Confederacy higher hopes on a different level. But Woodworth is certainly correct—harmonizing fully with observations made in *Why The South Lost the Civil War* and in the works of Paul D. Escott—that a crucial reason why there was such scant realistic chance for Southern victory was because few, very few, of the Southern people came even close to sharing Davis' degree of dedication to achieving Confederate independence.

Woodworth throughout displays keen insight concerning Jefferson Davis' qualities and limitations as a war leader. His personality, health, temperament and capabilities all combined with his limitations, and they constantly interacted. Despite possessing truly great assets, Davis also had some enormous flaws, and "One of his worst [was] a tendency to waffle under pressure" (p. 37). Another weakness was "proving that supply failures were someone else's fault was more important than a remedy for the situation" (p. 50).

But the foregoing is not to imply that Woodworth shows us too much of Davis and too little of Lee. Quite the contrary. As a brief aside, it may be interesting to some readers that Woodworth, while ignoring Tom Connelly's playfully suggested—but doubtless somewhat serious?—notion that perhaps Lee was a latent homosexual, Woodworth does point out that William C. Davis, in his recent biography of Jefferson Davis, went so far as to suggest that perhaps Judah P. Benjamin was one. . .any maybe not just a latent one either! (pp. 343n-346). Nor, for that matter, is this book at all entirely limited to insightful assessment of Davis and Lee. There is much food for thought concerning Joseph E. Johnston and Pierre Gustave T. Beauregard; and so too, the non-combatant General Samuel Cooper and various influential civilians—especially Judah P. Benjamin and John H. Reagan, the latter two cabinet officers being herein presented as quite active in military affairs and sometimes able as well as potent individuals who impacted on the overall war effort.

Woodworth's scholarship is wide, deep and profound, his documentation prodigious. His reading in both primary and secondary sources richly (and sometimes quite freshly) underpins his work. He is occasionally in surprising disagreement with some of the better modern scholars. This struck me quite sharply with respect to Woodworth's assessments of James Longstreet and Thomas "Stonewall" Jackson. If Woodworth is correct, then William Garrett Piston's fine and (to me) convincing thesis in *Lee's Tarnished Lieutenant* is overstated and flawed. Two other interesting interpretations offered by Wood-worth are: first, the Battle of Gettysburg was, indeed, the great "turning point"— a concept that I and others have denigrated, myself especially strongly in my most recent writings; and second, unlike Davis, whose mind-set was so completely different, Lee knew by the summer of 1864 that it was all only a matter of time—the South would never be able to lift or to survive the siege of Petersburg. Woodworth uses this almost as a throw-away transitional line, but it is an historiographically significant assertion that: "With the Union elections of 1864, the Confederacy's last flickering flame of hope finally guttered out once and for all" (p. 308).

Woodworth obviously reads and assesses with great care, and when he posits a disagreement, he does so in meticulous fashion—and with respectful reserve. Woodworth's writing is very satisfying. This is a long book but a delight to read. More important, it does what only much too rarely is achieved: it offers something of considerable value both to casual readers, buffs, and interested amateur Civil Warriors, as well as something for the most serious and deeply involved professional careerists in the field. Although he may not be quite the master synthesizer that William W. Freehling suggested is needed, in *The Reintegration of American History*, Woodworth has a commendable grasp of, and ability to integrate, not only a widely variant extant scholarship in the military field but also social and political aspects as well.

Herman Hattaway   University of Missouri-Kansas City

The History of the Harpers Ferry Cavalry Expedition, September 14 & 15, 1862, Allan L. Tischler (Five Cedars Press, 841 Wardensville Grade, Winchester, VA 22602), 1993. Maps, photos, notes, appendices, biblio., index. 345pp. HC. Contact publisher for price.

An increasing number of independent presses have been casting entries of late into the Civil War publishing field. Some have been well executed, useful works, particularly the reprints of older editions of books long unavailable to readers. Others have been less useful and of somewhat dubious quality, most of them in sore need of competent copy editing. Unfortunately this book leans mostly toward the latter description. It is especially regrettable because the author has compiled an impressive array of sources regarding the famous escape of the Union cavalry from Harpers Ferry prior to its capitulation on September 15, 1862. I would venture to say that he has left few stones unturned in his search for information. What he has not done, however, is weave that information into a comprehensive and enjoyable narrative. Though the author readily admits that his "paradigm" was "that of an anthology," and that the participants have been permitted to give "their versions" (p. iv), the overall result is less than satisfactory.

For reasons that remains unclear, Tischler has taken great umbrage to the way in which the story of the cavalry's escape from Harpers Ferry on the night of September 14 has been related over the years—both by participants and later historians of the campaign. He disparagingly labels their interpretation the "B. F Davis Saga" (p. iv). His motivation for writing this work was the realization that there were some "significant deviations" from the facts in those previous accounts (p. iv). He thus terms his book a "revisionist examination" and concludes with the hope that he has provided a more balanced view (p. 186).

In short, the crux of his complaint seems to be that Col. Benjamin F. (Grimes) Davis of the 8th New York Cavalry was unfairly handed the laurels after the episode, to the detriment of Col. Arno Voss of the 12th Illinois Cavalry, among others. It was Voss, the author points out correctly, who was named by Col. Dixon S. Miles as the commander of the cavalry force. Despite this evidence, it seems clear that Voss was merely the nominal commander whose seniority alone warranted the position. Davis, along with Lt. Col. Hasbrouck Davis of the 12th Illinois—competent soldiers both—were the instigators of the escape plan and determined to avoid the certain ignominy about to befall Miles and his troops. These men promptly became the de facto leaders of the expedition. Voss' later dismissal from the service as "not competent to command either a regiment or a brigade of cavalry" seems to support such a view (p. 158). At any rate, like any good story is wont to do, the tale of the gallant escape of the cavalry grew better with age until the embellishments sometimes swallowed the facts. Tischler seeks to reverse that process.

He begins with a capsule history of each cavalry unit involved in the escape, then moves on to examine in minute detail the various accounts surrounding the event. The book is divided into four parts: Prelude, Aftermath, Confederate Participant Accounts, and Union Participant Accounts. Since the section titled "Aftermath" includes extensive discussions dealing with the telegraph messages and newspaper articles about the cavalry's exploits, the bulk of the book could be said to be devoted to an examination of the myriad accounts of the escape. Though he correctly points out numerous inconsistencies in those accounts, they generally are of little real importance in the broader scope of events. As a result, the book often bogs down in a confusing discussion of minutiae that contributes little to the thesis and will likely leave the reader wondering what really happened. In addition, the general format of repetitive narratives—followed by a litany of errors found in each—becomes somewhat tedious, especially when there is no indication given of the significance of those discrepancies. All of this is compounded by the author's penchant for writing long, convoluted and improperly punctuated sentences. At times, Tischler seems to have been swept up in the style of the period, such as when he writes: "Inherent with that process was the remedy of corroborative delineation of sifting first-hand facts from second-hand repetitions, the latter being a narrative malignancy carried forward by numerous unsuspecting historians" (p. iv). Oddly, he goes on in the book to devote as much attention to the more easily discounted "second-hand repetitions" as he does to the more important "first-hand facts."

The book's strongest point is the amount of research that went into it. *The History of the Harpers Ferry Cavalry Expedition* is well documented and contains an extensive bibliography, although it excludes Paul R. Teetor's *A Matter of Hours: Treason at Harper's Ferry* (1982), one of the few full-length treatments of the debacle. Still, the work will be of great use in directing researchers to pertinent sources on this topic. The dramatic story of the cavalry's escape from Harpers Ferry continues to hold much fascination for readers, and it will undoubtedly continue to draw the interest of historians. Tischler's book should be the first place they turn for sources. As a comprehensive history of the Harpers Ferry cavalry expedition it is less useful. Whether or not his "revisionist" conclusions will be incorporated into future works remains to be seen.

Edward Hagerty   Glasgow, Virginia

Lee's Young Artillerist: William R. J. Pegram, by Peter S. Carmichael (University Press of Virginia, Box 3608 Univ. Sta., Charlottesville, VA, 22903-0608), 1995. Notes, maps, biblio., illus., index. 209pp. HC. $27.95

Colonel William R. J. Pegram was only twenty-three when he died, shot during an engagement at Five Forks only eight days before his beloved Army of Northern Virginia surrendered at Appomattox. Despite his youth, Pegram had risen through the ranks to become one of the most prominent artillerists in the Confederate Army. The "damn little man with the 'specs'" (p. 170) earned a reputation as a fearless combatant and profoundly changed the role of artillery in warfare. Peter Carmichael has written an ambitious study of Pegram's achievements, seeking to go beyond simple biography. Carmichael intends Pegram's life of morality, honor and religiously-inspired devotion to the Confederate cause to serve as a challenge to the loss-of-will thesis that has gained currency over the years as an explanation for Confederate defeat. Pegram and other young officers, Carmichael argues, viewed military service through the prism of religious duty: as representatives of a Godly nation they had an obligation to protect themselves from the invading Yankee horde. In return, God's favor would shine upon them, and bring their nation safely to independence. Thus Carmichael claims that these men comprised a core of true believers, prepared to do whatever was necessary to ensure the safety of their new nation. Pegram's beliefs and actions exemplified this commitment.

Willy Pegram was born in Richmond in 1841, the son of a successful banker. His father, James West Pegram, died in an 1844 steamship accident while on his way to visit his plantation holdings in Mississippi. Pegram's mother, Virginia, was forced to support her five children by teaching, and in 1855 established a girl's school in Richmond. The Pegram family was close knit and, fortunately for historians, wrote each other frequently, allowing Carmichael to base much of his biography on Willy's own letters. Following in his father's and grandfather's footsteps, young Pegram enlisted in a Richmond militia company in 1858 at the age of sixteen. He was in Charlottesville when the war began, however, pursuing his first year as a law student at the University of Virginia.

Pegram returned to Richmond in April 1861, rejoined his old militia company, and was almost immediately assigned to a new six-gun battery, the Purcell Artillery. Although initially only a temporary drillmaster, he was popular and efficient, and consequently elected to the office of second lieutenant. From that day forth Pegram was an artillerist and in that capacity saw action in almost every major battle in Virginia. He was promoted to captain (and therefore commander of the company) in March 1862. Although his battery was virtually decimated during the Seven Days fighting, the army applauded Pegram's "lust for combat" (p. 49), and he learned quickly from his mistakes. He was promoted three more times, eventually achieving the rank of colonel.

Carmichael is at his best when describing the many battles in which the Purcell battery participated, and he is well-aided by Theodore P. Savas' maps. Pegram was a fierce and fearless combatant, and he frequently risked his own life in order to spur on his men. His battery distinguished itself at Fredericksburg, Chancellorsville and at Gettysburg, where Pegram roused himself from his sickbed in Richmond and traveled by ambulance until he met up with his company at Cashtown on June 30. Not content with merely being at the battle, Pegram fairly begged his commanders to bring his battalion from the reserves to the front of the column, much to the chagrin of at least one of his men, who described the young officer as "rather too fond of fighting" (p. 97). The Purcell Artillery saw further action at the Wilderness, Cold Harbor and the Crater, where Pegram "considered it 'perfectly correct' to slaughter captured black soldiers 'as a matter of policy'" (p. 131). The battery spent the remainder of the war around Petersburg, sometimes in the trenches, occasionally engaging the Yankees outside the lines, until forced to retreat in early April 1865. During the Battle of Five Forks, Pegram remained mounted despite enemy fire, trusting in God to shield him, as he had done so many times before. Sadly, he received a mortal wound in his side and died shortly thereafter.

Perhaps it is better that Pegram died before Lee surrendered, for such an end to the war would have been hard for him to accept. Carmichael makes much of Pegram's courage under fire, his willingness to lay down his life for the Cause. Pegram's military valor grew out of his staunch religious convictions. He saw the world, in Carmichael's words, "through a prism of Christian duty." Therefore, "once Pegram enlisted in the army, he believed that he had made a contract not only with the Confederacy but also with God. Duty to God equaled duty to nation" (p. 5). Neither was a covenant that Pegram would break lightly, as he believed that "shirking combat constituted a serious transgression, one that violated duty to God, nation, community and family" (p. 170). Indeed, as the war entered its third year, Pegram came to feel increasingly isolated from a civilian population that he believed was unwilling to make the necessary sacrifices. Similarly, a gap had begun to emerge between Pegram and many of the men under his command who did not share their leader's seemingly insatiable thirst for battle.

The author does an excellent job of illuminating Pegram's ideology and attitudes. He quotes liberally from Pegram's own letters and from other descriptions of the artillerist. His explanation for the origins of Pegram's belief in a hierarchical Southern society is convincing, and his portrayal of the workings of the officer corps is a valuable contribution to the literature. However, Carmichael lacks enough convincing evidence to make his more ambitious larger point: that Pegram was one of a cadre of young Southern officers who shared his unswerving faith and loyalty. Consequently, the loss of will thesis needs to be reevaluated. Carmichael tries to make Pegram into an archetype even as he stresses his uniqueness. His attempts to extrapolate from one distinctive individual ultimately place too great a burden on the narrow shoulders of the young artillerist. Nevertheless, Carmichael's work provides a thorough and engaging tale of one man's coming of age on the battlefield.

Anne Sarah Rubin   University of Virginia

From Selma to Appomattox: The History of the Jeff Davis Artillery, by Lawrence R. Laboda (White Mane Publishing Co., Inc., 63 West Burd St., P.O. Box 152, Shippensburg, PA 17257), 1995. Maps, illus., biblio., end notes, index. 385pp. HC. $30.00

No sooner had the guns aimed at Fort Sumter ceased firing when communities from all over the South came forth with eager volunteers to join the newly created Confederacy. In the ensuing months after South Carolina took the lead in seceding from the Union, other states followed suit. Military units formed in various cities and towns across the South. One such community that reacted to the events of April 1861 was Selma, Alabama. In particular, an artillery unit named for their illustrious Confederate president, Jefferson Davis, would venture from Alabama and participate with the Army of Northern Virginia in most of the major campaigns of the Eastern Theater.

The story of the little known Jeff Davis Artillery is told by Lawrence R. Laboda, who relies on a wealth of unpublished manuscripts and primary sources. He provides an insight on the unit's activities and the men who comprised its ranks. Originally organized as a cavalry unit in June of 1861, the Jeff Davis Artillery reformed under this designation and mustered into the Confederate service a month later. The South was abundantly blessed with qualified horseman for cavalry units, but lacked men to form artillery commands. The battery spent most of its first summer training in Montgomery, Alabama and LaGrange, Georgia. The Alabamian's efforts to become skilled artillerymen were hampered by disease, which ravaged their encampment and depleted the ranks. Measles, mumps, diarrhea and dysentery took their toll because of unsanitary conditions in the camp. By the winter of 1861-1862, the company moved to Northern Virginia and camped near Centreville. Conditions were no better at this location, and the harsh Virginia winter contributed to the reduction of the company with disease continuing to take lives. Less than six months after its formation, the company was only at three-quarters strength. You get the feeling from reading Laboda's prose that only the Jeff Davis Artillery suffered from these problems. Of course, armies from both sides agonized about and suffered from filthy camps and general unsanitary conditions that resulted in sickness and death.

To make matters worse, the Jeff Davis Artillery also suffered from discipline and morale problems. From the moment they left Selma, discontent among the men was directed at their commanding officer, Capt. Joseph T. Montgomery. He proved to be incompetent as an officer and the men showed him no respect.

The morale of the company was boosted, albeit briefly, when Montgomery was court martialed, but a glitch in the hearing brought Montgomery back temporarily as commander. Five lieutenants from the company resigned in protest and Montgomery would eventually resign himself in February 1862. His replacements were not much better and the command structure of the unit suffered throughout the war.

During the spring of 1862, the Jeff Davis Artillery had the opportunity to forget the misery of camp life for a while, replacing it with the rigors of active campaigning. With the Confederate capital threatened by invading Union forces during the Peninsula Campaign, the battery, serving in Maj. Gen. D. H. Hill's Division, had their baptism of fire on the afternoon of May 31. The eruption of their guns signaled the start of the Confederate advance in the Battle of Seven Pines. Although the company sustained casualties in men and horses, the battery viewed its first battle as a success. According to Laboda, "the Alabamians had fought their guns well. Apparently, all the months of privation and sickness had failed to hinder the battery's effectiveness on the battlefield" (p. 27).

The following year brought little respite from the fighting, as the Army of Northern Virginia's new commander, Robert E. Lee, actively pursued the enemy. Conditions, however, were beginning to look up for the Jeff Davis Artillery. The battery's fire power was upgraded from howitzers to Napoleons. Even their health improved. Although still complaining about wretched food and poor camp conditions, the men were finally adjusting to life in the army. Their manpower shortage became a thing of the past, at least temporarily, as fresh recruits from Alabama filled the ranks almost to capacity. From an encampment near Fredericksburg, the Alabamians assisted Lee in thwarting attempts by the Union Army at Fredericksburg and Chancellorsville. The battery also played an active role during the Confederacy's unsuccessful invasions of the North at Sharpsburg, Maryland, and Gettysburg, Pennsylvania.

The battery performed well in these fights, but its role was mostly one of support. Laboda states that "there had not been any instance when the company, even when involved in a hot fight, had failed to provide an effective, if not destructive, supporting fire for the infantry" (p. 179). During the Battle of Spotsylvania, the battery was almost destroyed by a strong Union advance. By the close of the day's fight, three of its four guns were lost, twenty-two horses killed, forty members of the unit were casualties, and thirty more, including two senior officers, were prisoners. During the siege of Petersburg, the Jeff Davis Artillery was assigned a position on the James River near Richmond to drive off Federal gunboats. A portion of the unit was detached and sent to the Shennandoah Valley to assist Jubal Early's efforts against Phil Sheridan. When the war ended in April 1865, what remained of the unit from its inception was reformed to witness the surrender at Appomattox.

While the author leaves out few details about the company's movements and does a fine job of placing the unit's activities within the greater context of the war, occasionally the level of detail becomes tiresome. Laboda expends far too many words describing the constant reorganizations and promotions in the Army of Northern Virginia which, for the most part, had little effect on the Jeff Davis Artillery. Ultimately, this type of minutiae ends up causing confusion. In addition, Laboda's prose becomes labored when he insists on introducing new officers in rapid succession. Such information would be more useful and less of a drag on the story line if offered in the footnotes. The numerous maps—period and modern— photographs, and comprehensive rosters are a major plus. Despite the constant complaints of its members and significant internal strife, the Jeff Davis Artillery proved capable as a fighting unit and its story is one worthy of being told.

Mitchell Yockelson   National Archives

"Double Canister at Ten Yards": The Federal Artillery and the Repulse of Pickett's Charge, by David Schultz (Rank & File Publications, 1926 South Pacific Coast Hwy, Suite 228, Redondo Beach, CA 90277), 1995. Foreword. Photos, notes, 77pp. Paper. $8.00

Artillery Hell: The Employment of Artillery at Antietam, by Curt Johnson and Richard C. Anderson, Jr. (Texas A&M University Press, Drawer C, College Station, TX 77843-4354), 1995. Foreword, illus., appendix, index. 147pp. Contact publisher for price.

As Pickett's Charge reached the crest of Cemetery Ridge on July 3, 1863, a Confederate officer spied the three-inch rifles of the 1st New York Light Artillery, commanded by Capt. Andrew Cowan. The Rebel called for his men to take the guns, located just south of the famous cluster of trees, but Cowan acted first. Upon his order, his gunners unleashed a storm of canister at a distance of less than thirty feet, a deed memorialized in the grim phrase "Double Canister at Ten Yards" (p. 58). The effect on the thin gray line was devastating, and the Southern officer disappeared in the maelstrom of metal. The Confederates continued forward for only a few moments more before the survivors surrendered or turned to flee. Those that chose retreat were pursued across the open fields to Seminary Ridge by howling shells, just as they had been pounded by the Union batteries as they advanced a short time earlier.

The Battle of Gettysburg, including but not limited to the assault known as Pickett's Charge, has become the focus of an increasing number of micro-studies. Almost every minute detail of that clash has been closely scrutinized in scholarly and popular works of greatly varying quality. It seems almost impossible to agree with the introductory assertion of Charles Hathaway, a licensed Gettysburg battlefield guide, that "The role played by Union artillery at the Battle of Gettysburg has been long neglected" (Foreword). Nevertheless, David Shultz provides a detailed and well-paced, if brief, volume that illuminates the important role played by the big guns on that bloody field during the climax of the decisive battle in the eastern theater of the Civil War.

The author's terse style lends itself well to his narrative of the Union artillery operations on July 3, and he proves quite effective in conveying the tension of that harrowing afternoon. All of the heroes are here, from Maj. Gen. Henry Hunt, chief of artillery for the Army of the Potomac, to the youthful and ill-fated Lt. Alonzo Cushing, killed while serving his guns at the stonewall on Cemetery Ridge. There are new heroes as well, for almost every Union battery commander (as well as their men), emerges as an efficient practitioner of his chosen military vocation. It is made quite clear that the Southern bombardment preceding the attack had little or no effect, while the Union gunners played a vital role in disrupting the advancing columns with a variety of shells. As Lt. Tully McRea of the 1st United States Artillery later trenchantly observed, "Never was their [sic] such a splendid target for light artillery" (p. 53). The Federals skillfully pelted approaching grayclads at a distance, then raked the Rebel lines from the front and flank at close range, inflicting heinous casualties on their enemies.

Some 163 cannons from thirty-six Federal batteries assisted in the repulse of the Confederates. The author masters the daunting task of keeping the reader from becoming confused by the whirl of names and unit designations through the use of clear prose, several maps, and an order of battle for the batteries that actually engaged the assaulting regiments. For those unfamiliar with Civil War ordnance, a detailed glossary of terms is included, together with illustrations. This work does not contain a bibliography, and the footnotes are somewhat incomplete. As a result, some interesting paragraphs have no citations. Too, there is no index, which can be vexing for those interested in a particular person or unit.

A close scrutiny of the notes reveals that this study was written primarily from Union reports in *The War of the Rebellion: Official Records of the Union and Confederate Armies* (Washington, DC: United States Government Printing Office, 1880-1900), *The Bachelder Papers*, edited by David L. and Audrey J. Ladd (Morningside House, 1994), and the archives of Gettysburg National Military Park. These sources are supplemented by a handful of published unit histories, a like number of personal memoirs, and a half-dozen secondary works. Very few of these memoirs were written by Confederates, an interesting bias since certainly many such works must include some testimony about the effectiveness of the thousands of shells hurled at them. This entertaining little book, however, does not claim to be a definitive work, as guide Hathaway asserts that "it is only an overview, with much more to come" (Foreword). Apparently the author is preparing a more substantive work on the Federal artillery at Gettysburg. If the forthcoming publication is as clearly written as this initial study, it should prove to be a very useful and enjoyable volume for any serious student of the Battle of Gettysburg.

The Battle of Antietam on September 17, 1862, the bloodiest day of the Civil War, proved to be at least a partial success for the reorganized artillery of the Army of Northern Virginia. Assigned to battalions in order to concentrate their strength and enhance their impact, the Confederate batteries throughout the engagement protected Gen. Robert E. Lee's outnumbered infantry regiments in a superlative manner. Gaps in the thin gray lines were covered and Union assaults were repeatedly disrupted and driven back by a storm of canister and shell. By the end of the day, losses and the chaos of battle had forced a reversion to the older system of batteries operating on their own, but the point had clearly been made. Properly employed, artillery remained a vital component in the modern arsenal despite the introduction of superior infantry firepower through the use of rifled muskets. This lesson was underscored by the deadly work of the Federal artillerists, who inflicted heavy losses on their Rebel counterparts and at times drove them from the field with the accurate fire of their rifled fieldpieces.

The core of *Artillery Hell: The Employment of Artillery at Antietam*, a work focusing on Confederate and Federal gunners at Antietam, is a 1940 report by Maj. Joseph M. Hanson, a veteran of the United States artillery in World War I who was serving as a staff historian with the National Park Service. Assigned to compile a report on the actions of the many batteries at Antietam with an eye to moving some guns to the park as memorials, Hanson submitted a brief but thorough study. This included a discussion of the organization of the respective artillery forces, augmented with tables listing the number and type of guns for each battery; a detailed narrative of the employment of each unit as the battle developed; and an interesting list of the Confederate and Federal batteries ranked in order of their importance at Antietam. Hanson's report also contained logistical appendices indicating where guns might be found for the battlefield park in 1940 and how they might be distributed. Unfortunately, these have been lost and do not appear in this work. Hanson's study is both an expansion and revision of original battle reports and an update of the basic information provided by Jennings C. Wise in his 1915 study of the artillery of the Army of Northern Virginia entitled *The Long Arm of Lee*. Hanson does correct misinformation provided by those who fought at Antietam and by Wise, and his careful footnotes indicate the sources of his corrections.

The editors of this publication of Hanson's report include some useful information as a supplement to his work. A foreword by Edwin C. Bearss, former chief historian of the National Park Service, provides a brief biographical sketch of Hanson and a discussion of the historical context of his narrative. In 1940 there were no more than a handful of guns at Antietam, none of which were used to designate the site of an actual battery. Perhaps in response to Hanson's report, about three dozen more pieces were added within the ensuing twenty years. An explanation of the organizational situation before and during the fight at Antietam is crucial for understanding the events narrated by Hanson, and this is provided in a well-written essay by Curt Johnson, accompanied by present-day photographs of the battlefield taken by his daughter. Basic information about Civil War ordnance is found in a glossary written by Richard C. Anderson, Jr. Johnson and Anderson worked together to provide a line-by-line critique and expansion of the lists of Confederate and Union batteries compiled by Hanson. In this, they provide revised information about the number and type of ordnance for each unit, explain discrepancies between their figures and those of Hanson, and provide casualty reports, which Hanson did not do. An appendix recapitulates the numerical information in tabular form.

Bearss is correct that this slim volume is an "invaluable contribution" (p. xi) to understanding the crucial role played by artillerists at Antietam. One artilleryman later said that this fight was "artillery hell" (p. 7). The losses for Confederate batteries, which unlike a majority of the Union units were often exposed on the front lines, were particularly heavy. According to the numbers compiled by Johnson and Anderson, slightly less than 3.3 percent of the blue-clad gunners were killed, wounded or captured, while more than 9.6 percent of the Confederate gunners fell. Despite these casualties, both Rebel and Union artillerymen provided much-needed support at crucial points during the battle. While Hanson's assertion that the work of the Federal batteries proved to be the "decisive factor" (p. 55) that prevented a Confederate counterattack on Lee's left cannot be given full credence, it is true that the Union guns drove the enemy infantry back in several local counterstrokes. At the same time, Southern gunners stopped Federal assaults all along their line, buying time for the rapid movement of troops to meet the threats posed by superior numbers.

The value of this work lies in its juxtaposition of Hanson's report with information that was apparently not available to him. For Johnson's and Anderson's expansion of the earlier material on the Federal batteries, the pair rely principally on the papers of Henry J. Hunt, who became the commander of the artillery of the Army of the Potomac only a few weeks before Antietam, and those of Ezra A. Carman. Both of these collections are now housed in the Library of Congress. The updating of Hanson's Confederate lists was done through the judicious use of other portions of Carman's papers, reports in the *Official Records*, and some memoirs penned by participants in the battle. Johnson and Anderson also include a half-dozen after-action reports by Union officers, all of which are in the Hunt Papers and none of which have been previously published. All of this material, as well as Hanson's report, benefit from a thorough index, a sound bibliography, and a single map of the battlefield, which admittedly could show more unit positions or more of Hanson's landmarks as he discussed them in his narrative.

Nevertheless, this is a good presentation of an important study of Civil War field artillery at a key point in its development. As such, it should be of interest both to students of the "long arm" and those wanting a better understanding of the Battle of Antietam.

Richard B. McCaslin   High Point University

The Journals of Josiah Gorgas 1857-1878, by Sarah Woolfolk Wiggins (The University of Alabama Press, P.O. Box 870380, Tuscaloosa, AL 35487-0380), 1995. Foreword, illus., biblio., index. 305pp. HC. $39.95.

The immediacy and unique viewpoint of wartime eyewitness accounts have long fascinated Civil War scholars and buffs. Most accounts were written by common soldiers or ordinary civilians who recorded and reflected upon their experiences. Generally these chronicles ended with the war, as soldiers and civilians returned to what they perceived as rather uneventful peacetime lives.

Rarely did a major figure in the war keep a journal regularly; most published their recollections long after Appomattox.

Josiah Gorgas, the Confederacy's chief ordnance officer, was one of the few high officials who kept a record of his thoughts and experiences throughout the Civil War years. Born in 1818, Gorgas grew up in Pennsylvania and graduated from West Point in 1841. During the Mexican War, he served with Winfield Scott's army in the Vera Cruz campaign. While on assignment in Alabama in 1853, he married Amelia Gayle, the daughter of a former state governor. At the beginning of 1857 Gorgas started a journal to inform and inspire his children. When the Civil War began, Gorgas sided with his adopted state and was quickly appointed Confederate chief of ordnance, an office he held with great distinction throughout the war. After the collapse of the Confederacy, Gorgas struggled to make ends meet, seeking employment as a railroad official and unsuccessfully managing the Brierfield Iron Works for several years. In 1869, he accepted a position with the University of the South at Sewanee and became vice chancellor before leaving there to become president of the University of Alabama.

Frank E. Vandiver first published Gorgas' journals in 1947 in an edition that included only the Civil War entries and, out of deference to the feelings of Gorgas' daughters, omitted portions of the journals that had been defaced. Sarah Woolfolk Wiggins' comprehensive version prints all of the pre-war and post-war journal entries as well as the defaced passages. Wiggins' stated goal "is to allow the author to speak for himself to readers through a literal and readable text (p. xxix), and she succeeds admirably in *The Journals of Josiah Gorgas, 1857-1878.*

In his ante-bellum entries, Gorgas reflected on his hopes to settle on a plantation. He disliked the constant mobility of an army officer because he believed it would adversely affect his family. "I continually fancy how happy I could be with a spot of earth which I could call my own, which I could plant and improve. . . where I could live & die, & where some of my children might live & die after me" (p. 34). The threat of disunion, which Gorgas occasionally mentions, postponed his peacetime dreams. By June 1862, when he began the Civil War portion of his journals, Gorgas was in Richmond serving as chief ordnance officer of the Confederacy.

While they do not provide great detail or analysis, Gorgas' Civil War entries touch upon many subjects of interest to scholars. Although Gorgas remained hopeful of ultimate Confederate victory, his morale rose and fell with battlefield events. He occasionally questioned whether God had forsaken the South, but until the end of the war he retained his faith that God would save the Confederacy from its increasingly powerful foe. In early 1865, Gorgas noted that military events depressed many people in Richmond, but most young people maintained their joviality amid numerous weddings and engagements.

Gorgas offers candid commentary on military and civilian leaders. Much of it focuses on Confederate president Jefferson Davis, whom he criticizes for his strategic decisions and abrasive personality. The restoration of defaced passages reinforces Gorgas' low opinion of Davis. Nor do military figures escape Gorgas' biting tongue. In April 1863, when Major General Daniel H. Hill was before Washington, North Carolina, Gorgas notes reports that the enemy seemed concerned about Hill's presence. He wryly added, "Did they know Hill as well as we do they would be little alarmed. He can never achieve a success, tho' he might I suppose blunder upon one, as other short witted people do" (p. 62).

Gorgas' postwar entries are as illuminating as his Civil War commentary, providing a rare personal view of the South during Reconstruction. At war's end, Gorgas slowly made his way from Virginia to Alabama. Along the way, he noted the war's devastation and its effect on Southern white society. When staying with a "Mr. Webb" while traveling to Alabama, Gorgas offered a telling commentary: "Mr. W is a very wealthy man, or was, has a fine home, & a pretty married daughter, Yet he charged us $5. for our corn and entertainment. . . .People are so desirous of getting a little specie that they charge people entertaining them, a thing hitherto almost unknown, among the planters" (p. 172). Again, the restoration of defaced passages provides a greater understanding of the Reconstruction period by revealing Gorgas' personal depression, which ultimately resulted from the economic and material devastation of the postwar South.

The subject of black freedom often surfaces in Gorgas' postwar entries. He made a point to note the "smart" and "intelligent" individual freedmen he met who had no desire to take advantage of their new freedom. He seemed slightly surprised that the freedmen showed neither insolence nor insubordination. Gorgas believed that blacks gradually would be able to handle what he saw as the responsibilities of freedom, but he also believed that they would eventually disappear before the "moral & intellectual superiority of the white" (p. 205). He also discreetly offered a strategy to achieve the white dominance that occurred in slavery: "[w]here sense & discretion guide and direct the masters they will be sure to regain in time the sway, in some shape which they have at present lost, thro' the total failure of military operations" (p. 176).

Gorgas' journals are frustrating in some aspects. The scarcity of his reflections on his own department will disappoint students of Civil War ordnance. Only on April 8, 1864, his third anniversary as head of Confederate Ordnance, does Gorgas provide a brief assessment of his achievements in this department. Journal entries often are spread out, so that the immediacy of some events is lost because Gorgas reports them many days, and sometimes weeks, after they took place. These slight disappointments do not substantially weaken the journals' usefulness as an insightful primary account of one man's thoughts about the conflict and his struggles afterward.

Wiggins' edition of Gorgas' journals offers several new insights not present in Vandiver's earlier work. The added entries offer the reader a more intimate view of Gorgas and provide an important personal account of the Reconstruction experience in the South. The genealogy and biographical directory provided by Wiggins allow the reader to keep track of Gorgas' many close friends and relatives who move in and out of his journal entries. These features demonstrate the crucial importance of family connections in the nineteenth-century South. Wiggins' restoration of the journal's defaced passages does not significantly change Gorgas' Civil War accounts; they generally focus on criticism of generals and President Davis, and simply provide a more blunt description of faults that Gorgas chronicled more discreetly in the regular text. However, in the Reconstruction entries, the restored passages regarding Gorgas' depression add an important dimension to his account of the postwar South.

Wiggins succeeds in her goal of allowing Gorgas' journals to speak for themselves. The editing is not intrusive and does not interrupt his style or presentation. By including the entire date for each journal heading, the new edition makes it much easier to find specific passages quickly. But while Wiggins admirably fulfills the goal of allowing the journals to stand by themselves, the use of a few informational footnotes would have aided the novice student by adding context for some of the ideas and events that Gorgas mentions.

Despite this minor issue, Wiggins' timely update of Gorgas' classic Civil War account remains a valuable source for scholars and students of the Middle Period.

Jonathan M. Berkey   Pennsylvania State University

Gettysburg: July 1, by David G. Martin. Combined Books, 151 East 10th Ave., Conshohocken, PA 19428. Revised Edition, 1996. Maps, appendices, notes, index. d.j., HC. 736pp. $34.95

Students of the Civil War can and do argue ad nauseam whether the Battle of Gettysburg was the high water mark of the conflict. Such arguments are, of course, speculation, and thus not decisive. What is not in doubt, however, is that the three days of fighting in Pennsylvania has spawned more books, pamphlets, articles—and controversy—than any other engagement. Although the deluge of ink began shortly after the powder smoke wafted off the field, many of the finest studies have appeared in the last handful of years. Included in that stellar (but still relatively small) pantheon is a twin contribution from Harry Pfanz on the second day, three collections of essays, one for each day, all ably edited by Gary Gallagher, and Robert Younger's continuing excellent contribution via *The Gettysburg Magazine*, a quarterly periodical. Despite the fact that the first day's fighting set the stage for the two that followed—and consequently the stinging Confederate defeat that eventually took place—virtually nothing of import has appeared in book form. This oversight is due in large part to the heavier fighting that took place on the last two days of the battle, a series of bloodlettings that overshadowed the events of July 1. The only monograph approaching a serious study of the early hours of Gettysburg was Warren Hassler's *Crisis at the Crossroads: The First Day at Gettysburg*, printed more than a quarter century ago. Although it has played to a packed house for years, the book's many weaknesses—the most obvious its lack of a manuscript foundation—were obvious shortly after its appearance. Its ongoing popularity was largely the result of its stranglehold on the market, since no other similar volume, until now, was issued on the same subject. Competition has arrived in the form of David Martin's *Gettysburg, July 1*, which clearly supplants Hassler as the best single source on the first day of the fighting.

The first edition of Martin's study encountered several obstacles when it was apparently hurried to press with little or no editing. Predictably, the result was a book rife with errors, both textual and cartographic. Thankfully, Martin's publisher promptly issued a lengthy errata and has now printed a completely revised edition. This review is based on that revision.

It is far more difficult than one can imagine to research and coherently pen a book of this magnitude, especially one with this level of depth and detail. On balance Martin has succeeded in his mammoth endeavor, aided significantly by the book's sensible organization. *Gettysburg: July 1*, which offers a regimental examination of the day's events, follows the chronological sequence of the unfolding battle from the initial contact west of town to the collapse of the Federal XI Corps and the subsequent defense of Cemetery Ridge. The book itself is divided into nine lengthy chapters encompassing 559 pages of text, which are each in turn thankfully subdivided into smaller, more digestible, chunks. It is this latter method of presenting the large amounts of interesting and necessary minutiae in sub-titled sections that allows the reader to understand and appreciate each focused morsel before moving on to another naturally confusing and often interrelated event.

The general story of the fighting is well known and this is not the forum to rehash it. It is sufficient to acknowledge that Martin has a firm grasp of the complicated sequence of events and handles the difficult transition of attack and counterattack, arrival and retreat, smoothly and without noticeable difficulty. This reviewer particularly enjoyed the discussion of Robert Rodes' disjointed attack from atop Oak Hill and the author's handling of the devastation that befell Iverson's Confederate brigade. No doubt readers will be pleased that Martin does not shy away from the multitude of controversies and mysteries that permeate every battle, including the death of John Reynolds, who fired the first shot, and which Federal corps collapsed first, to name just three.

Martin's writing style is generally easy to follow and appreciate, although his use of military time (1300 for 1:00 p.m., for example), is needlessly distracting. The other troublesome element of *Gettysburg: July 1*, comes at the end of the book, where Martin includes a subsection entitled "If Jackson Had Been Present" (pp. 563-569). Discussing objective differences in the Army of Northern Virginia brought about by Jackson's death is perfectly acceptable (the army's altered organization and its effect on combat operations, for example). Sheer speculation, however, is something else altogether. While enticing, it is better handled over a pint of ale and bowl of peanuts than in a work of this magnitude. The author makes several missteps in this regard when making definitive (or speculative) statements as to what Jackson would have done. For example: ". . . Jackson *certainly* (reviewer's emphasis) would not have held the troops that constituted Pender's division out of action all morning. . . ." (p. 564); "Jackson would *probably* (reviewer's emphasis) have disregarded Smith's concerns. . . ." (p. 565); Jackson would *probably* (reviewer's emphasis) have made an attempt to capture Cemetery Hill or Culp's Hill. . ." (p. 565). Martin compounds this questionable excursion into the realm of conjectural discussion by going on to evaluate the best Confederate route of attack late on the afternoon of July 1—as discovered by wargamers. Although this reviewer himself enjoys computer military simulation games, even the suggestion that such models adequately and accurately replicate events on a battlefield (not to mention taking into effect the human element) and thus have any application to historical events, is dubious at best. This type of discussion, which weakens rather than bolster's Martin's credibility, has a proper place; it is not in *Gettysburg: July 1*.

The author's generally smooth-flowing prose is supported by twenty above-average maps, although they vary in quality vis a vis attempted coverage. Although they are better than most that accompany a typical battle account, the style employed takes some careful scrutiny to follow and comprehend. The overall strategic illustrations are more confusing and difficult to understand than the tactical selections, primarily because unit names often are abbreviated and troop designations appear in both line and a variety of block formations. In addition, some of the maps, ostensibly inserted to clarify complex accompanying discussion in the text, require lengthy legends to decipher. For example, "Map 13" on page 348 contains a legend with twenty-two abbreviations: "ALM" stands for "Almhouse," a physical structure; "HW" is "Herbst Woods," a natural stand of timber; and "FOR" is "Forney," a farm, and so on. These caveats aside, the maps are by and large useful in following the fighting and readers will appreciate their inclusion.

In addition to his micro-specific coverage of the battle's events, Martin thankfully provides a detailed order of battle (Appendix I); a table of divisional-level casualties (Appendix II); a discussion of the topographical aspects of the field (Appendix III); a discussion of both chronological and meteorological issues (Appendix IV); Medal of Honor Winners (Appendix V); and battery armaments (Appendix VI). The author's end notes are an added bonus, a wealth of additional information that serious readers will find both useful and interesting.

It is difficult to dispute that Martin's *Gettysburg: July 1* is now the standard source for the first day's fight. It strengths outweigh its several, but relatively niggling, lapses. Many Gettysburg enthusiasts—and they are legion—have known for a long while that the first twenty-four hours of the conflict were every bit as fascinating, momentous and heartrending as the forty-eight that followed. Martin has now proved it.

Theodore P. Savas   San Jose, CA

BOOK NOTES

Battery Wagner: The Siege, The Men Who Fought and the Casualties, by Timothy Bradshaw, Jr. (Palmetto Historical Works, 120 Branch Hill Drive, Elgin, SC 29045). Photos, maps, notes, biblio., appendices, index, 249pp. HC. $33.50

Although *Battery Wagner* was published some three years ago, it was not widely reviewed and consequently is not as well known as it should be. The topic is especially appropriate given the subject theme of this issue of *Civil War Regiments*.

This study is actually two books in one: the story of Battery Wagner, and a collection of appendices containing various information on the men and siege. The first segment, a history of Wagner, details its construction and the men who attacked and defended the bastion. The narrative is well-written and competently researched, with end notes supporting the text. While there does not appear to be any groundbreaking new material, Bradshaw covers the mini-campaign in depth and offers a significant amount of detail not found elsewhere. This portion of the book is also well-illustrated, with some rare views of various earthworks. The handful of maps are adequate in following the text.

The second segment, 119 pages, includes casualty lists for virtually every man injured in the assaults on the fort, with many stating the location of the wound (ankle, leg, hand, etc.), vignettes on various aspects of the mini-campaign (which lasted 58 days), and a fascinating surgeon's report.

Anyone with a serious interest in Charleston and the complex Federal campaign to capture the city will find this book of substantial interest.

From Huntsville to Appomattox: R. T. Cole's History of the 4th Regiment, Alabama Volunteer Infantry, C.S.A., Army of Northern Virginia, edited by Jeffrey D. Stocker. (University of Tennessee Press, Knoxville, TN 37996-0325). Maps, photos, end notes, biblio., index. Cloth. $32.95

Another fine volume in the Voices of the Civil War Series. Jeffrey Stocker, a Pennsylvania attorney and longstanding student of the war, has edited and made available an excellent narrative account from a member of one of the premier fighting regiments of the Army of Northern Virginia. Regimental adjutant R. T. Coles served with the 4th Alabama from First Manassas to Appomattox, and was thus especially suited to record the unit's history. His service also included a stint in the Western Theater with James Longstreet, which provides his history with a full-bodied flavor that is difficult to top. His observations of other officers, the regiment's battlefield service, and the internal politics and strife of a Confederate regiment make for an excellent read.

Stocker's detailed end notes are a treasure trove of information and wonderful minutiae, perfect for both the casual student and the information-crazed Civil War bibliophile. While Cole's manuscript is accompanied by a fine gallery of quality photos (many of them quite rare), the two theater maps do not do justice to the overall product.

Historian Edwin C. Bearss endorsed this book as "a fourfold barnburner." He was not exaggerating. Anyone interested in either Lee's army or Confederate regimentals should own this book.

Advance and Retreat: Personal Experiences in the United States and Confederate States Armies, by John Bell Hood. (University of Nebraska, Bison Books edition, 1996). New introduction by Bruce J. Dinges. Maps, frontis photo, paper, 358pp. $15.00

A facsimile reprint of General Hood's memoirs. While the title suggests otherwise, this volume is primarily a recollection of his Confederate service. *Advance and Retreat* contains some interesting firsthand accounts, although it is essentially an attempt to explain away his battlefield failures by rebutting Joe Johnston's own recollections, which condemn Hood's Civil War record. Hood was a sour, crippled man by the time he got around to writing his version of the war. Readers must be careful, as the old general salted his narrative with misleading statements, half-truths and outright lies. The new introduction is well-written and interesting.

Recollections of the Civil War, by Charles A. Dana. (University of Nebraska, Bison Books edition, 1996). New introduction by Charles E. Rankin. Frontis photo, index, paper, 296pp. $12.95

Newspaperman Charles Dana, who acted as the War Department's eyes and ears at the front (i.e., a spy for Edwin Stanton), witnessed many of the war's most memorable moments in the Western Theater, including David Porter's running of the Vicksburg batteries, the siege of Vicksburg, the collapse of the

Union army at Chickamauga and the successful assault against Missionary Ridge. His candid descriptions of many of the war's prominent Union generals, coupled with his keen eye for detail, make this a book worth owning. Originally printed in 1898. Rankin's introduction is detailed and informative.

From the Cannon's Mouth: The Civil War Letters of General Alpheus S. Williams, edited by Milo Quaife (University of Nebraska, Bison Books edition, 1996). New introduction by Gary W. Gallagher. Photos, map, index. 405pp. Paper. $15.00

On of the true classic letter collections of the war and one of *Civil War Magazine's* 100 best Civil War books. Williams served in both the Eastern and Western Theaters as a brigade, division and corps commander. His varied experience under a wide array of commanders is carefully detailed in this compendium, which was first edited by Milo Quaife and originally printed in 1959. Strong in detail on military operations and the internal workings and mechanizations of army politics. Williams' accounts of his service with the Army of the Potomac are truly memorable. This edition includes a fine introduction by Gary Gallagher. Bison Books was thoughtful enough to leave Quaife's original introduction in this new edition.

SOFTWARE REVIEW

The *Official Records* on CD-Rom

More historians, researchers and even general students of the war reach for *The Official Records of Union and Confederate Armies* than any other set of published records. And for good reason. No where else will you find in one collection more reports, correspondence, casualty lists, and other important primary material than the *Official Records* (or as it is more commonly referred to, the *OR*). Access to this mammoth set of 128 individual volumes plus the index has to date posed a significant problem for many researchers. Just finding a complete set is not always an easy task since relatively few individuals own it. In addition, not all libraries possess (or display) them, in large part because the thirty-some feet of shelf space required for display often makes owning a set impractical. The computer age has solved several of these concerns, for now the entire set of *OR* is being offered for sale on CD-Rom by three separate publishers at essentially the same time. While not everyone owns a computer, and fewer still own one with CD-Rom capability, the number of these machines available is growing. I must admit I enjoy holding and browsing through the books themselves. There are few things finer in life than cracking open a new book and enjoying the wonderful scent of a freshly printed page. Thus, the thought of using a computer to dig into a reference set that I have sitting on a nearby shelf was not initially appealing. Being a lover of the physical product I have not, by and large, changed my mind, although the ability to pop in a disk and conduct a thorough search offers significant advantages and is also an enjoyable process.

The publishers that have submitted their product for review are: Broadfoot Publishing Co., of Wilmington, NC; H-Bar Enterprises, of Oakman, AL; and Guild Press, of Indianapolis, IN. Both Broadfoot and Guild stressed that their products were advanced prototypes and subject to some changes, while H-Bar's was a finished piece of software. While all three versions were found to be professionally packaged and handsomely presented, they varied in their ease of usefulness, availability of special or enhanced features, and accuracy.

All three software packages were clear and easy to read on the screen and scrolled smoothly through the material. All three possess point and click icons as well as drop-down menus, which make it easy for the user to access the available options and resources offered by the software. Since it is impossible in the limited space available to fully review every feature of all three packages, I have decided to offer a brief discussion as to how each package functioned generally, before focusing on a few major features that most users will find of interest in determining whether to purchase this reference set on disk, and if so, which to acquire. I examined all three packages within a Windows95 environment using a Pentium 133mhz machine and 32 mb of ram. No obvious system conflicts were observed.

The first package I examined in-depth was the prototype offered by Guild Press, which contained the majority of the *OR* volumes. Guild's gray and blue screen is divided into two portions (left and right), with the viewing screen on the right, and an index tree / root system on the left. The respective screens can be easily sized to the convenience of the user with the mouse, and various search windows may be opened at the same time. The *OR* are listed in the left window by serial number, although the standard method of citing this set is by the actual volume number and not the serial number. I wanted to access vol. 27, pt. 2, p. 18 (Gettysburg reports), for example, and experienced some minor delays until I figured out that serial 44 was the volume I needed. By using the point and click method, I chose this serial and was rewarded with a second window below the first listing 100-page sections and the reports contained in this volume, arranged by number. Each section contained a "page jump table" spanning 100 pages ("topic breaks," as the publisher calls them). Clicking on this table produced a calendar-like table with each page denoted. Clicking on the page sent me where I wanted to go. The Guild prototype allows for "simple" text searches (which seeks out exactly what you typed), and "complex" searches (which employs searches using "near," "or," "and," and "not.") Other searches can be launched within certain fields, such as the signer of reports, the addressee, or the date of the writing. My simple search for "Dan Tyler" resulted in numerous search possibilities listed in the left lower window by serial volume (in this case No. 44, for example), with the "hits" showing up on the right side of the screen highlighted in black. Clicking on an arrow button on the top strip menu sent me forward or backward to each strike, although I could not determine how many "Dan Tyler" strikes had been found by the Guild search engine. Guild's prototype also offers the user a breakdown by "Great Battles" and "Significant Court martials/Inquiries."

I next examined Broadfoot's prototype, which contained only the three Gettysburg volumes. This package, also with a primarily blue and gray interface, contained one large screen with a top button strip and drop down menu options. Searches are initiated by clicking on a flashlight icon, which pops up a box with all the commands on a single screen, including search operators (and, or, not, near, within, and a pair of parentheses), a comprehensive indexed word wheel for use as a search guide, and a current field guide (main, text, or header). By typing in "Dan Tyler," the search engine kicked out a two line message that read: "82 Serial No. 44 Series I Vol. 27, Part II—reports," which means that there are 82 separate references to "Dan Tyler" in vol. 27, pt. 2. The second "hit" line evidenced an additional 56 strikes in vol. 27, pt. 3. Clicking on the first line took me to the title page of vol. 27, pt. 2, while a click on either of a pair of yellow arrow buttons took me forward or backward through the listings, with "Dan Tyler" highlighted in yellow. The individual page breaks were in blue text and easy to see.

The last of the three I examined was H-Bar's product, which also contained the three Gettysburg volumes. H-Bar's software, also with a blue and gray interface, is designed with the point and click buttons arranged along the left side of the screen and drop down menus across the top. Clicking on the query button popped up a screen with a box within which to type the search text, an indexed search wheel, and an "infobase" scope guide, which lists numerous search fields similar to Guild's. Typing "Dan Tyler" brought up a page of text on the screen with the words highlighted in blue. At the bottom of the page were three small ribbons listing the record number "14322/59404," the number of hits as "1/66" (meaning the first of sixty-six, although Broadfoot's had discovered 138) and "Query: dan tyler." Cycling through by clicking on a pair of black arrow buttons took me to the Tyler strikes. Individual report headings are reproduced in bright purple.

While all three versions are based on allowing users to search using key words, Broadfoot's is also equipped with what it calls "hypertext," a function that allows the user to search for words highlighted with a mouse. This proved to be a very helpful attribute. Guild's provides a similar feature by allowing users to highlight words, copy to clipboard, and paste into the query field. All three packages allow for proximity searches ("Hood and Lee within 25 words" for example), although it appears that such searches in Guild's prototype are conducted only within individual reports or correspondence and not across the entire *OR*.

After operating all three for some time, it became apparent that all three packages operated with similar principles and methods, similar interfaces, and without significant differences. This is not to say that the packages are indistin-guishable, for they are surely not. Since the *OR* is usually referenced for re-search purposes as opposed to poolside reading—and therefore cited in scholarly studies—the ease of citation will be a major concern to users. When this set is only visible on a computer screen, and page by page at that, is it simple to determine which volume, part (several volumes are broken into two or more "parts," or separate books), and page number you are viewing? This threshold inquiry revealed the first substantive difference in the three products.

While both Broadfoot and H-Bar clearly denote which page a reader is on, only Broadfoot's has the complete citation (series, serial number, volume, part, and page), at the top of every page in bright blue lettering, which is easy to see. H-Bar reproduced the headers printed at the top of each original *OR* page, but these citations provide only the page number and chapter—but not the volume or part, critical information you need in order to properly cite from the *OR*. As it turned out, the information as to volume and part was available in H-Bar's version. I had to scroll up and down several pages to find it, however, because it is printed, like the text itself, in black, which makes it hard to locate. Similarly, Guild lists the volume and part number in a static window at the top of each page, but this window does not include the page number the user is on. Instead, the page number, substantially smaller than the surrounding text, is embedded in the text of the page itself and surrounded by brackets thus: [657]. This rather cumbersome method of pagination forces the user to comb the page for a very small page number that I found difficult to locate. No one wants to spending precious research time just trying to figure out which page (or volume and part) you are searching.

The precision of reproduction from book to computer disk is another aspect I spent considerable time examining. I selected several pages at random from each software package and compared them to the printed page. Let's take vol. 27, pt. 2, p. 18 as an example. Two of the publishers—Broadfoot and Guild—impressed me with their completeness and accuracy. I could not find a mistake in either's version. H-Bar's package, however, had the most errors in transcription (be it electronic or manual). While some were of the niggling variety, several were of a more serious nature. For example, on the page cited above, there were a half-dozen of what I would consider minor but troubling errors (extra spaces in front of commas, "3, 30 o'clock" instead of "3.30 o'clock"; the letter "m" standing alone as a separate word in the middle of the text where none exists in the original version; and the word "the" dropped from the middle of a sentence). Substantive inaccuracies, obviously more serious than those heretofore mentioned, were also present in sufficient number to raise significant reservations. For example, H-Bar's version reproduces Thomas A. Maulsby's name as "Maulby" several times on page 18, although it is spelled correctly on page 19. Similarly, the One Hundred and Twenty-Sixth Ohio (126th Ohio) is noted as "Once hundred and twenty-sixth Ohio"; "throw" is spelled "thrown," and "on our front with at least a brigade. . ." is reproduced as "on out front witch al least a brigade." These types of errors denote hasty and sloppy editing. While several pages of H-Bar's software I examined did not have any errors (as one would hopefully expect), the number of them found on this single page alone would force me, as a researcher, to double-check substantive citations in the original set of books. This step, of course, defeats most of the purpose of owning the software in the first place. If you can't confidently depend on the software to reproduce the original *OR*, can it be used for research and citation purposes? It is also interesting to note that, (as near as I could tell), paragraph breaks in both the Broadfoot and Guild versions mirror exactly those found in the printed *OR*, while H-Bar's does not. Thus, the five separate paragraphs that appear on vol. 27, pt. 2, page 18 are reproduced in H-Bar's package as one long paragraph. This is important if someone wants to cite a long passage in quotation.

The transcription and presentation of information formatted into tables, such as casualties and strengths, also varies considerably between these three publishers. The importance and usefulness of the data found in tabular form, which speckles the *OR* landscape only somewhat less frequently than meteor craters on a barren lunar body, cannot be overstated. Thus, the manner of its presentation on the computer screen is of no little importance. I randomly selected the single margin-to-margin table found in vol. 27, pt. 1, p. 294 as an example. Both Broadfoot and Guild reproduce it, like the original, as a single table, while H-Bar breaks it into two separate tables, one for officers and the other for enlisted men. Of the three, Broadfoot's method of displaying tabular data is clearly superior to its competitors in view of its ease of understanding and printing. It appears to have been retyped and re-formatted (as was Guild's) using a standard legend (k=killed, KO=killed officers, etc.), so that it would fit, like the original, as a single table. The major difference between Guild's and Broadfoot's is that Broadfoot's table easily printed out onto a single page of paper, and printed exactly as it appeared on the screen. Guild's version ran off the right margin (albeit slightly). Although Guild's version is slightly cramped and not as attractive or instantly intelligible as Broadfoot's, both are accurately reproduced with regard to the information contained thereon. H-Bar's version printed fine, but the two-table formatting system makes it much more difficult to understand. Of more importance is the disappointing fact that the figures under the columns denoting casualties for the officers and enlisted men were not properly lined up. Thus, an unsuspecting user might run afoul of some Pennsylvania Gettysburg buff when claiming that Paul's First Brigade lost 35 officers killed at Gettysburg on July 1, when in fact the original table claims but a single such casualty. This type of formatting error is a serious problem because it renders the table worthless. Lastly, the original table contained a brief footnote denoted by an asterisk (*). All three publishers reprinted the footnote text (and reprint footnote and explanatory items found throughout the *OR*). Both Broadfoot's and H-Bar's appear, as in the original version, on the page itself. Guild employs pop-up text boxes that are accessed via asterisks (*) with the mouse button.

While they are often not particularly good, the original *OR* has dozens of maps that are useful when thumbing through the reports and correspondence. It is natural to expect that these maps would be available in these computer versions of the *OR*. Only two of the three publishers, Broadfoot and Guild, reproduced them; H-Bar's package does not offer any maps at all, a strange oversight. Of the two versions available for comparison, the differences were relatively minor but worth noting. Take, for example, the full-page map found in vol. 27, pt. 1, p. 915. Guild chose to print the map (apparently the same size as the original) sandwiched between two blocks of text, thus it will only print with the

surrounding text. While this is not a serious flaw, it is not an accurate repre-
sentation of the original version. Broadfoot's presentation, while more faithful to
the original, is not perfect either. Although printed as an entire page, it is not clear
what page, for citation purposes, the map is on. Broadfoot's programmer prom-
ises that this oversight on the prototype will be corrected for the final version.
Both publishers thoughtfully enhanced the original maps by allowing a user can
zoom in and out on each map by clicking on the right button on the mouse, which
makes it easier to read some of the fine print. Guild's used gray scale scans,
which makes it easier to read small text on enlarged maps, while Broadfoot's
monochromed scans appeared a bit jagged in this regard. Broadfoot's has two
additional features designed to allow users better access the *OR* maps. The first is
a skipping mechanism so a user can jump back and forth from map to map
(without intervening text) by simply clicking on a camera icon found at the top of
the page. The second is the added feature of allowing the user to rotate the image
in 90 degree increments. These last pair of features make Broadfoot's offering in
this regard better than its counterpart, although overall Guild's presentation is
virtually identical.

Attempting to actually print selected on-screen material also developed significant differences between the three software packages. All three have simple
point and click printing functions, but selective printing was only possible with
two of the three packages (Broadfoot's and H-Bar's). In other words, a user can
simply highlight a single word, sentence, paragraph or page and print that selection. With Guild's prototype, however, there is no option to print selected text
within the *OR* software package. A user thus has two choices: print the entire
topic selection (several pages long), or highlight a slice of text, paste it into a
separate word processing program, and than print the selection from that piece of
software. Given the obvious time, effort and expense that Guild has spent developing its prototype, this extra step is an irksome (and unusual) formatting quirk.

While all three programs allow users to easily copy text and paste it into
another document (Word Perfect or Microsoft Word, for example), Broadfoot's
package includes what it calls an "electronic notepad," a separate window-based
system which allows users to copy, paste, add their own "marginalia," or notes,
and save for later use (or print into a hard copy version), all without having to
rely or use another word processing program. Guild's includes a "bookmark"
feature that permits a hierarchical bookmark list to be made. This data is stored in
a single file which can be exported and printed with another application. I could
not find any way to do anything similar with H-Bar's product

While I have tried to focus on several key areas that will hopefully interest potential users and purchasers of these important products, there are other custom features that deserve mention. The most important of these are offered by Broadfoot. According to their computer representative, they entered "thousands" (their number) of corrections and additions, all of which are presented in *italicized* text throughout the OR. These corrections include such things as spelling errors, errors in rank, and so on, while the additions might offer a middle name where only an initial (or nothing) was available in the past. Also, if a user wants to jump to a specific page in a single step, as far as I can determine, only Broadfoot's search engine allows you to do so by specifying the volume and page number. While all three versions are based on allowing users to search using key words, Broadfoot's is also equipped with what they call "hypertext," a function that allows the user to search for words highlighted with a mouse.

The cost of this software is not inexpensive. Guild's has the lowest retail cost at $450, which includes Dyer's three-volume *Compendium* and Fox's *Regimental Losses,* two very helpful and welcomed sources on CD-Rom. H-Bar's price for the full set was the highest at $750, although you can purchase individual battles (1-5 books, depending on the battle, on one disk), for about $50.00 each. These are placed on a recordable CD and can be mixed with several other offerings, including *Jefferson Davis: Constitutionalist, Rise and Fall of the Confederate Government,* to name just two. Broadfoot's full set of the *OR* is $600.00, although it offers a $200.00 credit toward the 100-volume *OR* Supplement on CD-Rom with the purchase of this initial offering. The *Supplement* is 100 or so volumes of reports and correspondence that did not get into the original *OR*. Broadfoot also claims it will have several Civil War scholars "scrutinize" the first edition of its software for mistakes, and that it will send, free of charge, an updated version to everyone who purchases this first edition. While I have not seen it, Broadfoot will offer a complete printed and bound user's manual with its finished product. Guild will apparently offer a scaled down version and rely more on its on-line assistance, while H-Bar does not offer any printed instructions. All three software packages offer on-line help, and all three offer a money back guarantee.

Is it worth purchasing the *OR* on CD-Rom? After several hours of experimentation with all three packages, the advantage of sitting in one chair and searching the entire *OR* with a global search engine became increasingly obvious. Printing hard copies with the click of a mouse (as opposed to lugging heavy books to a copier and plugging the thing with nickels), coupled with the ability to send valuable information into your favorite word processing format (i.e., pasting text directly into your manuscript) are just two major reasons why all serious researchers will have to have a full set of the *OR* on CD-Rom. Although it takes getting used to, digging into the *OR* on disk will eventually prove faster, easier and cheaper than using the printed version. I hesitate to say that using the mammoth 128 volumes is now outdated, since it is a question of taste and long years of habit. The real battlefield of this war between these three publishers is a question over the custom features each offers (or doesn't offer) and the accuracy of translation. Each potential purchaser will have to decide for himself which options are more important for his own particular purposes.

Theodore P. Savas   San Jose, CA

INDEX

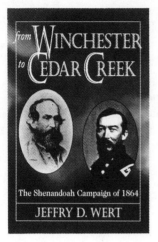

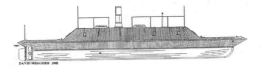

CAPITAL NAVY:

The Men, Ships and Operations of the James River Squadron, by John M. Coski,

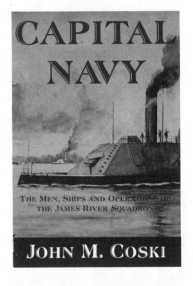

Finally, a rich and fully documented history of the important service rendered by the men and ships of the James River Squadron, whose role in defense of Richmond shaped the course of the Civil War in Virginia. Dr. John M. Coski, the historian with The Museum of the Confederacy, has spent years mining manuscript collections for unpublished letters, journals, diaries and reports. Basing his study on these primary source materials, many of which have never been used before, Coski has weaved a compelling account of Richmond's development into the naval capital of the South, and how her citizens, politicians and military establishment crafted, against heavy odds, the most powerful naval squadron to sail under the Confederate banner.

Capital Navy's fast-paced narrative carries the reader from the May 15, 1862 Battle of Drewry's Bluff, where the Rebels repulsed a powerful Federal naval thrust just a handful of miles below Richmond, through the stunning climactic battle sequences in Trent's Reach in January 1865. The face-to-face engagement with the Federal monitor *Onondaga* in Trent's Reach crushed Southern hopes for a naval victory in Virginia. Less than three months later, the James River Squadron hastened its own end with gunpowder and Southern torches, extinguishing forever the Confederacy's only "capital navy."

Sandwiched between Drewry's Bluff and Trent's Reach were the grueling years of torpedo and mine warfare that immobilized the vast resources of the United States Navy. *Capital Navy* introduces students of the Civil War to the officers, sailors and civilians that designed, built and launched the mammoth ironclads, and provides a detailed examination of Richmond's two river-based shipyards. In addition to offering exhaustive coverage of the careers of the iron warships, Coski sheds considerable light on the heretofore overlooked service rendered by the gallant wooden ships that fought alongside their more famous iron sisters, discusses the Confederate Naval Academy and its training facilities, the James River submarine mystery, and much more. The Civil War in Virginia cannot be fully understood without reading this book.

Specifications: Six maps by Mark A. Moore, 13 original blueprint-style drawings detailing every ironclad of the James River Squadron, 77 photographs and illus., many previously unpublished; End notes, appendices, biblio., index, 50-lb. acid-free paper, d.j., cloth, 343pp. ISBN 1-882810-03-1. $29.95 ($4.00 shipping)

"The research and writing is balanced, exciting, and timely. . . .Savas Woodbury has scored another major coup with *Capital Navy!*"

Edwin C. Bearss,
noted Civil War author and former Chief Historian for the National Park Service

---

Savas Publishing Company
1475 S. Bascom Ave., Suite 204, Campbell, CA 95008

Order Toll Free: 1-800-848-6585

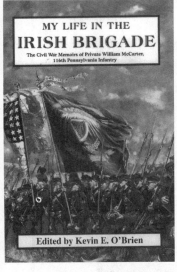

Fort Fisher
Illustrated

The Photographs of T. H. O'Sullivan

By Chris E. Fonvielle, Jr.

Featuring thirty-six photographs of Fort Fisher (twenty of which are previously unpublished) and fifteen modern photos, all keyed to twelve stunning maps by cartographer Mark A. Moore. Includes complete narrative history of both battles for Fort Fisher. 144pp, notes, biblio, index. Cloth, d.j., ISBN: 1-88281022-8

$19.95

Summer 1997

Savas Publishing Company
1475 S. Bascom Ave., Suite 204, Campbell, CA 95008

Order Toll Free: 1-800-848-6585

The Civil War and American Society

June 22-28, 1997

A seminar sponsored by the George Tyler Moore Center for the Study of the Civil War

You are invited to learn about the effects our nation's bloodiest conflict had on the common soldier, on the communities located near the battlefields, and on the families that the soldiers and sailors left behind.

The seminar includes lectures on the Southern press, the U.S. Marines at the Battle of 1st Manassas, the 5th New York Infantry at 2nd Manassas, Maryland Confederates at Gettysburg, Sharpsburg's citizens in the aftermath of Antietam, the 20th Maine *before* the Battle of Gettysburg, West Virginia's Union widows and the federal pension system, and photography at Antietam.

Battlefield tours include First and Second Manassas and Second and Third Winchester. Optional tours also are available to Gettysburg, Antietam, Harpers Ferry or Monocacy.

Our featured presenters include Brian Pohanka, Tom Desjardin, David M. Sullivan, Hannah N. Geffert, Ted Alexander, Thomas Clemens, William Frassanito, and Richard McMurray—this year's Scholar-in-Residence. John Hennessy and Todd Kern will lead our battlefield tours.

Registration is $499 for a "resident" attendee and $299 for a "commuter" attendee. Please contact us for complete seminar details and a registration form.

GEORGE TYLER MOORE
CENTER FOR THE STUDY OF THE
CIVIL WAR

Shepherd College
Shepherdstown, WV 25443
Voice: (304) 876-5429
E-mail: gtmcweb@shepherd.wvnet.edu
World Wide Web: www.shepherd.wvnet.edu/gtmcweb/cwcenter.htm

Shepherdstown is located on the banks of the Potomac River 5 minutes from Antietam Battlefield

The Civil War and American Society

June 22-28, 1997

A seminar sponsored by the George Tyler Moore Center for the Study of the Civil War

You are invited to learn about the effects our nation's bloodiest conflict had on the common soldier, on the communities located near the battlefields, and on the families that the soldiers and sailors left behind.

This year's seminar includes lectures on the Southern press, the U.S. Marines at the Battle of First Manassas, the 5th New York Infantry at Second Manassas, Maryland Confederates at Gettysburg, Sharpsburg's citizens in the aftermath of Antietam, the 20th Maine Regiment *before* the Battle of Gettysburg, West Virginia's Union widows and the federal pension system, and photography at Antietam.

Battlefield tours include 1st and 2nd Manassas and 2nd and 3rd Winchester. Optional tours also are available to Gettysburg, Antietam, Harpers Ferry or Monocacy.

Our featured presenters include Brian Pohanka, Tom Desjardin, David M. Sullivan, Hannah N. Geffert, Ted Alexander, Thomas Clemens, William Frassanito, and Richard McMurray—this year's Scholar-in-Residence.

Mary Tyler Moore (left) presents the keys to the Conrad Shindler House – home of the George Tyler Moore Center for the Study of the Civil War – to Center Director Mark Snell, May 1996.

Registration is $499 for "resident" attendee and $299 for "commuter" attendee. Please contact us for complete seminar details and a registration form.

GEORGE TYLER MOORE
CENTER FOR THE STUDY OF THE
CIVIL WAR

Shepherd College
Shepherdstown, WV 25443

Voice: (304) 876-5429
E-mail: gtmcweb@shepherd.wvnet.edu
World Wide Web: www.shepherd.wvnet.edu/gtmcweb/cwcenter.htm

Shepherdstown is located on the banks of the Potomac River 5 minutes from Antietam Battlefield